# Searchlights fc
# Year 3 Teache

## Chris Buckton    Pie Corbett

# Contents

| | | | |
|---|---|---|---|
| *Introduction* | | | iii |
| *Scope and Sequence Chart* | | | vii |
| **Term 1** | Unit 1 | 'Long' vowel phonemes and sounding out | 2 |
| | Unit 2 | Adding ing | 4 |
| | Unit 3 | le endings | 6 |
| | Unit 4 | Common prefixes | 8 |
| | Unit 5 | Making opposites | 10 |
| | Unit 6 | Spelling strategies | 12 |
| **Term 2** | Unit 7 | Vowel phonemes **or**, **er** and **air** | 14 |
| | Unit 8 | Adding er, est and y | 16 |
| | Unit 9 | Spelling plurals | 18 |
| | Unit 10 | Compound words and apostrophes | 20 |
| | Unit 11 | Silent letters and apostrophes | 22 |
| | Unit 12 | Common suffixes | 24 |
| **Term 3** | Unit 13 | More 'long' vowel phonemes and sounding out | 26 |
| | Unit 14 | More spelling strategies | 28 |
| | Unit 15 | Words in words and homonyms | 30 |
| | Unit 16 | Prefixes | 32 |
| | Unit 17 | More prefixes | 34 |
| | Unit 18 | More apostrophes | 36 |
| Additional Unit 1 | | Counting syllables and spot the error | 38 |
| Additional Unit 2 | | Even more spelling strategies | 40 |
| Additional Unit 3 | | Learning spellings and proofreading | 42 |
| *Facsimile Big Book pages* | | | 44 |

## CAMBRIDGE UNIVERSITY PRESS

CAMBRIDGE UNIVERSITY PRESS
Cambridge, New York, Melbourne, Madrid, Cape Town, Singapore, São Paulo, Delhi

Cambridge University Press
The Edinburgh Building, Cambridge CB2 8RU, UK

www.cambridge.org
Information on this title: www.cambridge.org/9780521891790

First published 2002
6th printing 2008

Printed in the United Kingdom by Polestar Wheatons

*A catalogue record for this publication is available from the British Library*

ISBN 978-0-521-89179-0 paperback

ACKNOWLEDGEMENTS
The publishers would like to thank the following
for helping with the trialling of *Searchlights for Spelling*:

Abbotsmead Junior School, Cumbria
Ashbrook First School, Milton Keynes
Braniel Primary School, Belfast
High Bentham CP School, N. Yorks
Manorbrook Primary School, Bristol
St Richard's RC Primary School, Chichester
Watton-at-Stone Primary School, Herts

Barrow Community Learning Partnership (EAZ), Cumbria

Illustrations by Patrice Aggs, Robin Lawrie and Rachel Merriman.

Cover background photograph of coral reef: Kelvin Aitken/A.N.T./NHPA
(Natural History Photographic Agency)

Design and layout by Pentacor plc.

# Searchlights for Spelling

*Searchlights for Spelling* is a comprehensive spelling scheme for Years 2–6/Primary 3–7 that covers all the word-level spelling objectives of the National Literacy Strategy (NLS) and meets the requirements of the National Curriculum.

It is a systematic scheme for teaching the patterns of the English spelling system through stimulating, multi-sensory activities. It builds up spelling concepts through an investigative approach, equipping children with the skills to tackle new words as well as developing their strategies for the recall of key words and spelling patterns.

The scheme also builds on NLS programmes such as Progression in Phonics (PiPs) and Spelling Bank and is cross-referenced to them, making use of their basic interactive techniques such as 'Get Up and Go', 'Show Me', and 'Time Out' (see Key terms overleaf for further explanation).

## Spelling for writing

The reason for learning to spell is to become fluent in everyday writing. *Searchlights* is designed to equip children to write fluently, rather than simply to learn and be tested upon decontextualised lists of words. It aims to make spelling enjoyable, through developing a sense of curiosity about words and an awareness of language patterns.

The sessions begin by deepening children's *understanding* of an objective or strategy, through direct teaching or investigation. This is followed by *applying* their understanding through shared writing and independent activities. It is important to ensure that spelling objectives are always emphasised in the children's own writing, in order to reinforce the concept of spelling for a purpose.

## A multi-sensory approach

The activities are based on four key learning styles:

- visual – remembering common patterns; writing words down to check whether they 'look' right; looking at the 'tricky' bit and trying the letters in a different order; looking for words within words; seeing the word in your mind, holding a word in your memory by seeing it, then looking to the top left of your mind to recall.

- aural and oral – hearing and pronouncing words; emphasising or exaggerating pronunciation to aid learning (e.g. *Wed-nes-day*); breaking words into syllables or phonemes; remembering some words with a rhythmic strategy (e.g. *Mrs d*, *Mrs i*, *Mr ffi*, *Mr c*, *Mr u*, *Mrs lty*: *difficulty*); using rhyme to spell by analogy.

- kinaesthetic – writing common patterns; tracing over words; sky-writing as you say each letter; getting the feel of common handwriting joins.

- cognitive – knowing rules, conventions, possible and impossible combinations; identifying word roots, suffixes and prefixes; using knowledge of grammar (e.g. ed – past tense), using mnemonics (e.g. *there is* a rat *in sep*arate).

By experiencing a multi-sensory teaching approach, children who learn in different ways have every chance of developing their ability to spell. Good spellers use a range of strategies. The whole class and pupil activities in the scheme use a variety of approaches. To further support multi-sensory teaching, the above symbols are given next to the quickfire activities for each unit – Oddbods and Snip-snaps (see Key terms, page iv).

## Identifying and representing phonemes

*Searchlights* generally follows the NLS Framework conventions for identifying and representing phonemes, including the use of 'long' and 'short' to distinguish certain vowel phonemes. For the most part *Searchlights* adopts other NLS terminology. Phonemes are represented by bold type in all materials, while letter patterns are red in the Teacher's Book, Big Book and Pupil's Book and underlined in the Photocopy Masters Book.

It is important to note that the teaching of certain phonemes and their associated letter patterns can be affected by regional variation in pronunciation. You will need to adapt your teaching of these phonemes to suit the needs of your class. Such instances are noted in the relevant units.

## Spelling practice – little and often

Children need frequent practice so that spelling becomes automatic and does not interfere with the act of composition. *Searchlights* is designed to be as flexible as possible and can be used in a variety of ways, depending on the needs of the children. The activities fit naturally into word-level work within the literacy hour and have a simple, regular pattern. They can be adapted for different classes and groups.

## Spelling and handwriting

*Searchlights* emphasises the important link between spelling and handwriting, particularly in Year 3. Regular practice of handwriting joins helps to consolidate the learning of common letter strings. A joined script is offered wherever it is intended that a child will copy or continue writing.

## Spelling log

It is helpful for children to develop the habit of keeping a personal spelling log. It can contain:

- collections of words arising from the independent activities;
- lists of oddbods (see Key terms below) and other 'tricky' words;
- results of spelling investigations;
- dictations and other tests;
- personal spelling targets;
- useful strategies or mnemonics;
- space for **Look Say Cover Write Check** practice.

A possible format for a spelling log is included in the Photocopy Masters Book for those who want to make use of it. Reference pages in the Pupil's Book, and extra pages in the Big Book, also provide useful material which the children could transfer to their log.

## How to use *Searchlights for Spelling*

### Key terms

| | |
|---|---|
| **Brush-ups:** | activities which revisit objectives from the previous year, for those children who need more time to catch up. |
| **Catch-you-out:** | a word that is an exception to a specific rule or teaching point (e.g. where a word changes completely when forming a plural rather than just adding s or es). |
| **Get Up and Go:** | individual children come out to the front to demonstrate something. |
| **Oddbod:** | a 'tricky' word that causes common difficulties (featured on the Big Book left-hand page and in the list of words to learn in each unit). |
| **Time Out/ Show Me:** | all children can respond by writing on dry-wipe boards and showing the spelling attempt. |
| **Sky-writing:** | drawing the shape of a letter or word in the air as an aid to memory. |
| **Snip-snaps:** | short, snappy ideas for further practice in applying the unit's objective or in learning key words. |
| **Spelling log:** | a personal ongoing record of words being learnt (see Photocopy Masters Book page 13). |
| **Think about... / Extra challenge:** | both these suggestions take the children a little further in exploring or applying a spelling concept. |

### Colour-coding

Red type is used to highlight target letters and letter patterns. To highlight phonemes and distinguish them from spelling patterns, they are printed in bold type.

(In the Photocopy Masters Book, where colour is not used, letters and letter patterns are underlined and phonemes are in bold.)

# The components

For each year there are four key components:

- ▦ **Teacher's Book** – containing a double-page spread of step-by-step notes for each unit's teaching as well as background information.
- ▦ **Big Book** (or OHTs for Years 5–6/Primary 6–7) – containing a double-page spread of whole-class material for each unit as well as useful revision and supporting material.
- ▦ **Pupil's Book** – containing a double-page spread of differentiated activities for each unit and reference pages with word lists and reminders of spelling rules and strategies.
- ▦ **Photocopy Masters Book** – containing a photocopiable homework copymaster (PCM) for each unit as well as revision activities, assessment material and guidance for parents.

Together these resources provide 18 core units of work for the year (six units a term). Three additional units provide further material, which can be fitted in as necessary. Each unit comprises two parts:

- ▦ Part 1 – introduces the spelling objective(s).
- ▦ Part 2 – takes the objective(s) one step further, or introduces a further objective, and provides a test dictation.

## Part 1

**Teaching the objective(s):** Swift, lively interactive teaching of objective(s), using the left-hand page of the Big Book, plus teaching of key words, including 'oddbods' (see Key terms).

**Using the objective(s):** Developing the skill or concept through writing, including brief opportunities for shared writing.

**Independent work (Pupil's Book):** Differentiated activities focusing on reinforcement and extension of target objectives (see Differentiation, following). This may take place as part of a literacy hour, or at another time.

**Review (plenary):** Review of independent work and recap of main teaching points.

**Homework:** Reinforcement task generally with an investigative element which can involve other family members; words to learn for the unit's dictation.

## Part 2

An extended whole-class session.

**Teaching the objective(s):** Usually revisiting and developing the unit focus, using the right-hand page of the Big Book.

**Using the objective(s):** Writing with the class, pausing and discussing spelling points.

**Review (plenary):** Review and summary of new learning, and discussion of homework findings.

**Follow-up homework:** This allows for further exploration or reinforcement of learning.

**Test dictation:** Class dictation that includes examples of the spelling objective and oddbod(s) for the week.

## Differentiation

Independent activities in the Pupil's Book are differentiated at three levels, A, B and C. A and B activities consolidate children's learning of the key objectives of the unit, while C activities are more challenging or address a further objective. C activities may anticipate Part 2. Children could work through all three when appropriate. The Extra challenge in some units extends children's learning further.

Children who find spelling particularly difficult may need extra time to revisit key objectives from the previous year or years. For Year 3/Primary 4 children who need extra phonics teaching, use activities for the earlier steps in the NLS Progression in Phonics (PiPs). *Searchlights* also provides a bank of Brush-up ideas based on the previous year's objectives as well as six extra revision PCMs.

For each unit, the words to learn list on the homework PCM is differentiated (A, B, C) so that some children can be given fewer target words to learn.

## Paired spelling

Children could spend ten minutes every day following this simple procedure in order to learn their individual lists (between five and ten words at a time). This procedure could also be introduced to parents and it is given as part of the 'How to help your child with spelling' guidance (see Photocopy Masters Book, pages 47–48).

- The child reads the word; says it aloud; spells the letters out; tries to spell it out without looking.
- Together, parent/partner and child discuss 'tricky bits' and devise a way of remembering them.
- If the child finds the word hard to remember, repeat the first two stages as necessary before attempting to write.
- The spelling partner/parent covers the word.
- The child writes it down.
- Together they check – if incorrect, revisit two or three more times.

## Assessment

The units include a dictation test, as well as a termly SATs-style test to track progress. To be useful, spelling tests should always be diagnostic. Look carefully at the results to find out what strategies the children are using. It is important, too, not to penalise them for incorrect but intelligent, plausible guesses. One useful approach is to allocate two marks to each word: the first mark could be given if the target phoneme, pattern or rule is correct (e.g. *ai* spelt correctly in *rain*) and the second if the whole word is correct.

A simple Tracking sheet to help you monitor children's progress is provided in the Photocopy Masters Book (pages 3–5). Children's involvement in assessing their own progress in spelling is very important. To encourage children to review their own learning, yearly self-assessment sheets with 'I can' targets are also provided (see Photocopy Masters Book, page 14).

## Test dictation

The object of regular dictation is to give the children practice in spelling words in context, reinforcing the importance of accurate spelling in writing.

*Searchlights* dictation provides three levels of differentiated sentences for each unit. The children learn the words before they are tested on some of them in context. In Year 3/Primary 4 there are ten words to learn per unit: comprising words related to the unit's objective(s); wherever possible words are drawn from the NLS list of high frequency words; the oddbod(s).

Test scores and comments can be recorded on the teacher Tracking sheet (see Photocopy Masters Book pages 3–5). The suggested procedure for the test dictation is as follows.

### Introduction (first unit)
- Explain to the children what a dictation is.
- Tell them that you will be dictating sentences.

### Procedure
- Tell them that first, you'll read the whole sentence while they listen. Specify whether you want them to write out the whole sentence or just the target word.
- Then explain that you'll read a little bit at a time while they write it down (if they are writing out the whole sentence).
- Tell them what to do if they come to a word they don't know: try to break the word up into its sounds, or think of another rhyming word which perhaps they can remember how to spell.
- Give prompts where appropriate, e.g. reminding them of rules or asking questions such as: *Remember that oddbod? Listen to that word again – what sound can you hear?*
- Read each sentence through again so that they can check their writing.
- Note: Make sure that you do not expose strugglers. Children should simply write the words they have learnt (A, A/B, A/B/C). There is no need to draw attention to difference here.

## Homework

For each unit, a homework PCM provides the related list of words to learn for the dictation test and a task that reinforces the unit's teaching, or focuses on revision. The sheets also encourage an investigative approach. Words to learn for each unit are offered in three levels of difficulty. They are referred to as key words in the Photocopy Masters Book and listed there in full on page 6.

Parents/carers are offered further guidance on a separate PCM: 'How to help your child with spelling'.

# Scope and sequence chart – Year 3

| Unit | NLS Objectives | Big Book | Pupil's Book | Homework PCM | Snip-snaps | Oddbods |
|---|---|---|---|---|---|---|
| 1 'Long' vowel phonemes and sounding out | NLS 3.1.W1, W2, W6 | 'Long' vowel phonemes and sounding out | Creating rhyming strings; Finding common endings; Creating word chains | Investigating 'long' ai | Robot Voices Robot Segmentation Joining Letters | put |
| 2 Adding ing | NLS 3.1.W8 | Adding ing | Sorting, changing and labelling | Word sort – adding ing | Which Box? Rhyming Pairs Eyes Closed | was |
| 3 le endings | NLS 3.1.W9 | le endings | The le Families | Crazy rhyme | Quickfire Rhymes Adding ly Who-hoo | they |
| 4 Common prefixes | NLS 3.1.W10, W12 | Common prefixes | Sorting and changing words by prefix; defining dis | Prefix sentences | Play 'Beat the Clock' Find the Prefix Joining Up | are, our |
| 5 Making opposites | NLS 3.1.W11, W12 | Making opposites | Creating opposites; Separating prefixes from their roots | Prefix rewrite | 'Beat the Clock' Again Finding Roots Quick Write | moment |
| 6 Spelling strategies | NLS 3.1.W6 | Spelling strategies | Word towers | Jog your memory | Seeing It Writing It Hearing It | out |
| 7 Vowel phonemes or, er and air | NLS 3.2.W1 | Vowel phonemes or, er and air | Finding and sorting or, er and air words | The or sound | Thumbs Up, Thumbs Down Listening Game Rhyming | girl |
| 8 Adding er, est and y | NLS 3.2.W8 | Adding er, est, and y | Calligrams; Writing sentences; Creating a poem | Adding er and est | Big, Bigger, Biggest Even Bigger Adding y | first |
| 9 Spelling plurals | NLS 3.2.W9, W11 | Spelling plurals | Sorting plurals; Changing plurals to singular and vice versa | What happens to words that end in the letter o | Quickfire Plurals Plural Practice Perfect Your Plurals | last |
| 10 Compound words and apostrophes | NLS 3.2.W12, W15 | Compound words and apostrophes | Making compound words; Breaking up compounds and writing sentences | Compound jigsaws | Compound Words Make It Informal … And Formal Again | clue |
| 11 Silent letters and apostrophes | NLS 3.2.W10, W15 | Silent letters and apostrophes | Silent letters | Silent crossword | Shhh Letters Make it Informal … And Formal Again | answer |
| 12 Common suffixes | NLS 3.2.W13, W14 | Common suffixes | Spelling endings ly, er, ful, less | Word pools | Change the Gender Quickfire Oddbod Beat the Clock | lovely |

vii

# Scope and sequence chart – Year 3 cont.

| Unit | NLS Objectives | Big Book | Pupil's Book | Homework PCM | Snip-snaps | Oddbods |
|---|---|---|---|---|---|---|
| 13 More 'long' vowel phonemes and sounding out | NLS 3.3.W1, W2, W6, W8 | More 'long' vowel phonemes and sounding out | Letter patterns oi, oy, ai, ay; Alternative spelling of the 'long' vowel phoneme ai | Words within words | Hear It<br>See It<br>Say It | help |
| 14 More spelling strategies | NLS 3.3.W6 | More spelling strategies | Rhyming words | Word partners | Does It Look Right?<br>Taking a Picture<br>Hear It | water |
| 15 Words in words and homonyms | NLS 3.3.W8, W14 | Words in words and homonyms | Hidden words | Word hunter | Quickfire Spelling<br>What's the Meaning?<br>Spot the Hidden Word | wood |
| 16 Prefixes | NLS 3.3.W9, W10 | Prefixes | Hunt the word – prefixes mis, co, non, ex, anti | Spot the prefix | Creating New Words<br>Prefix Charades<br>Quickfire Writing | your, you're |
| 17 More prefixes | NLS 3.3.W10 | More prefixes | Combining prefixes and root words | Cracking prefixes | Quickfire Questions<br>Change the Meaning<br>How Much? | school |
| 18 More apostrophes | NLS 3.3.W11 | More apostrophes | Rewriting contractions | Apostrophe chatter | Write in Full<br>Quick Contractions<br>Finding Oddbod Rhymes | push/pull |
| Additional 1 Counting syllables and spot the error | NLS 3.1.W4, W5 | Counting syllables and spot the error | Joining syllables; Working out the number of syllables | Sorting syllables | Isolating Syllables<br>Sort Out the Letters<br>Spot the Error | even |
| Additional 2 Even more spelling strategies | NLS 3.2.W6 | Even more spelling strategies | Word spiders for prefixes/suffixes | Spelling sets | Change the Word<br>Letter I-Spy<br>Anagram Hangman | next |
| Additional 3 Learning spellings and proofreading | NLS 3.3.W5, W7 | Learning spellings and proofreading | Building words | Acrostics for spelling | Does It Look Right?<br>Word Squares<br>Anagrams | when |

| YEAR | TEACHER RESOURCE | WHOLE-CLASS TEACHING | PUPIL RESOURCE | HOMEWORK REINFORCEMENT ASSESSMENT |
|---|---|---|---|---|
| Y2 | Teacher's Book | Big Book | Pupil's Book | Copymasters |
| Y3 | Teacher's Book | Big Book | Pupil's Book | Copymasters |
| Y4 | Teacher's Book | Big Book | Pupil's Book | Copymasters |
| Y5 | Teacher's Book | OHTs | Pupil's Book | Copymasters |
| Y6 | Teacher's Book | OHTs | Pupil's Book | Copymasters |

# 1 'Long' vowel phonemes and sounding out

| **Objectives for Unit 1** |
| Revision of **ai**, **ee**, **ie**, **oa**, **oo**; segmenting |

## Part 1

**You need** Big Book page 2; coloured pens; dry-wipe boards or notebooks in pairs; Pupil's Book pages 2–3; PCM 1

**Whole class**

- Introduce the objectives: looking at different ways of spelling 'long' vowel phonemes, and practising segmentation ('sounding out').
- Begin with some swift oral segmentation. Say a CVC word (*cat*) then ask the children to break it into its smallest sounds – or use phoneme 'fingers': holding up fingers corresponding to the number of sounds they can hear – before sounding aloud together. Progress to words with consonant clusters, e.g. *cash*, *dish*, *rich*, *tricks*, *stops* etc.
- Look at the BBk page. Ask the children to say the words and listen to the vowel phonemes. 'What is the difference in the middle vowel phoneme?' (*Cat* and *got* have 'short' vowel phonemes; *cane* and *goat* have 'long' vowel phonemes.)
- Read through the poem together then discuss how to segment the underlined words. Isolate the 'long' vowel phonemes. Tell them to say each word slowly and then 'talk like a robot' – break it up before writing down the sounds they can hear.
- List on the board common spelling patterns for 'long' vowel phonemes **ai** (ai in *brain*, a-e in *name*, ay in *play*) and **oa** (oa in *boat*, o-e in *pole*, ow in *blow*).
- Make up silly sentences together using the different spellings for each phoneme. Segment the relevant words, isolating each phoneme to aid spelling, e.g. *The* **s-n-a-ke** *and the* **s-n-ai-l** *went to* **p-l-ay**. *The* **g-oa-t** *sent a* **n-o-te** *to the* **c-r-ow**.
- Introduce the oddbod: *put* – see below.

**Pupil activities**

A: Write rhyming words.
B: Find the most common ending when the phoneme **oa** ends a word.
C: Create word chains.

Think about ...: Listening to the sounds of words.

**Review**

- Ask the children to tell you what they have learnt about segmentation. Ask them to recall the ways of spelling the 'long' vowel phonemes **ai** and **oa**.

**Homework**

Investigate which is the most common way of spelling the 'long' vowel phoneme **ai** at the end of a word.

---

**Oddbod** put ◉ ⊖
- Write up *put* and *poot*. Children put thumbs up for which looks right.
- Depending on local pronunciation, list rhymes or other words that share the same pattern, e.g. *cut*, *shut*, *but*.
- Say sentences using the word, but instead of saying the word chant the spelling, e.g. *I am going to* p-u-t *it on the table*.

**Snip-snap** Robot Voices ♪ ⊖
- Ask the children to act like robots (arm out, moving from left to right), and sound out words with 'long' vowel phonemes, e.g. *tray, tree, tea, try, pie, glow, so, blue, flew, paid, pane, sleet, eye, soap, tone, true, soon*.
- They chant – you write the spelling. Keep this swift.

2

**NLS objectives for Unit 1**

3.1.W1    3.1.W2    3.1.W6

## Part 2 | You need    Big Book page 3; coloured pens; dry-wipe boards or notebooks in pairs

**Whole class**
- Recap: **ai** and **oa**. Chant the 'long' vowel phonemes together: **ai**, **ee**, **ie**, **oa**, **oo**.
- Look at the BBk page. Children read the words, using blending where appropriate, then match the pictures to the words.
- Together, make a list in the table of the most common ways to spell the 'long' vowel phonemes **ie**, **ee** and **oo**.
- Time Out/Show Me: Ask the children to think of more words to add to the lists. 'Which seem to be the most common ways to spell the different sounds?'

**Review**
- Recap the most common ways to spell the 'long' vowel phonemes **ai**, **ee**, **ie**, **oa** and **oo**.

  **ai** snail, a-e snake, ay tray;
  **ee** sweet, ea seat;
  **ie** tie, i-e mine, igh sigh, y cry;
  **oa** soap, o-e phone, ow crow;
  **oo** moon, u-e tune, ew stew, ue blue.

- Homework review.
- Make a list of all the words you can remember that end with the **ai** sound. Point out that ay is the most common ending.

**Follow-up homework**
- As a reminder, ask children to draw a small picture next to each spelling for the 'long' vowel phonemes **ai** and **oa**:

  snail    ai    drawing of snail;      soap    oa    drawing of soap;
  snake    a-e   drawing of snake;      crow    ow    drawing of bird;
  tray     ay    drawing of tray;       phone   o-e   drawing of mobile phone.

**Test dictation**
- OB  I put on my red jumper and scarf.
- A   A snail is very slow. The white cat had a brown tail.
- B   How far can Jim throw the ball? I took a note home from school.
- C   We always go out at the weekend.

---

**Snip-snap**  Robot Segmentation
- Focus on 'long' vowel phonemes **ai** and **oa**.
- You say a word and the children chant like robots, segmenting the sounds.
- Then they sound it out to themselves and write the word on dry-wipe boards.

**Snip-snap**  Joining Letters
- Show Me: Children write down *said* on dry-wipe boards rapidly, joining letters.
- Ensure aid is joined.
- Tell them to chant *said* = s-a-i-d as they all write.

# Adding ing

To add ing, dropping e and doubling final consonant

## Part 1

**You need** Big Book page 4; two different-coloured pens; dry-wipe boards or notebooks in pairs; Pupil's Book pages 4–5; PCM 2

**Whole class**

- Introduce the objective: what happens when we add ing onto a word.
- Look at the BBk page and read the words through. Point out the two different things that happen when you add ing to a word (just add ing or drop e and add ing).
- Ask children to tell you what has happened to the spelling of each of the words. Together, sort them into two groups.
- Get Up and Go: a volunteer circles all the examples where the main verb doesn't change, e.g. *jump – jumping*.
- Another volunteer circles all those verbs where the final e is dropped, e.g. *smile – smiling*.
- Write funny sentences for words ending in ing, emphasising the rule, e.g.
  - *I was looking at the smiling clown.*
  - *I was asking the amazing pirate.*
  - *I was driving the jumping kangaroo!*
- Children contribute by writing ing words on their boards.
- Introduce the oddbod: *was* – see below.

**Pupil activities**

A: Sort words – just add ing/remove final e.
B: Sort words – 'short' vowel just before the final consonant – double the letter when adding ing.
C: Remove ing and writing the root word.?

Think about ...: Adding ing.

**Review**

- Recap on words that don't change and words that drop the final e when adding ing.

**Homework**

Sorting words that just add ing from words that drop the final e.

---

**Oddbod** was 💭 📝
- Remember this by using the mnemonic '**w**hat **a s**wot!'
- Ask: 'On dry-wipe boards, who can write it correctly the most times in 20 seconds?'

**Snip-snap** Which Box? 👁 👂
- Draw two boxes on a board, labelled 'add ing' or 'drop e'.
- Say a word that just adds ing (*pick, sing, call, jump*) or that ends in e (*give, starve, rave, wave*).
- Children give the thumbs up or down, to show which box the word should go in.

---

**NLS objective for Unit 2**

3.1.W8 (See Spelling Bank page 4)

---

## Part 2 | You need      Big Book page 5; coloured pens; dry-wipe boards or notebooks in pairs

**Whole class**
- Recap – when adding ing, some words do not alter, and those ending in e drop the e.
- Look at the BBk page and draw lines from words to the relevant postbox.
- Explain that words with a 'short' vowel phoneme just before the final letter double the final letter, e.g. *slip – slip*ping.
- Show Me: Ask children to add on ing and jot down spellings on dry-wipe boards for each type.

**Review**
- Children tell one another what they have discovered about words with a 'short' vowel before the final letter, e.g. *run – run*ning.

- Homework review.
- Make a brief list of verbs that describe things the children have done so far today, and add ing to each one. Highlight the rules used in each case.

**Follow-up homework**
- Children collect a list of 30 words that have had ing added to them. Which is most common – just to add ing, to drop the e, or to double the consonant?

**Test dictation**
- OB  The cow was brown, black and white.
- A    The boys were diving into the pool. Mum and Dad were smiling kindly.
- B    The fireworks were amazing. The cars were slipping down the hill.
- C    Jan and Bill were queueing in the shop.

---

**Snip-snap**   Rhyming Pairs
- Generate rhyming pairs with a 'short' vowel, e.g. you say *hop* – they say *shop*.
- Show Me: Children write each word, adding on ing.
- Check they double the final consonant.
- Try *chat/bat, clap/rap, plan/fan, slip/rip/nip/whip/trip.*

**Snip-snap**   Eyes Closed
- Write a NLS key word in the top left-hand corner of the board so that the class are looking up and to the left. Try: *two, were, want.*
- Ask them to 'take a picture' of the word, close their eyes and see it.
- Say: 'Hold it there – now jot it down. Who can write the word the most times in 20 seconds?'

# 3  le endings

## Part 1

**You need**  Big Book page 6; two different-coloured pens; dry-wipe boards or notebooks in pairs; Pupil's Book pages 6–7; PCM 3

**Whole class**

- Introduce the objective: learning the spelling pattern le. Note that words which end in vowel-l-'magic' e are specifically excluded from this objective, as the le does not form a separate syllable.
- How do you spell *little*? Jot these down on a board and point to each one: *littol*; *littel*; *littal*; *litterl*; *little*
- Say: 'Thumbs up for the correct one – which 'looks' right?'
- Look at the BBk page and match the pairs of rhyming words by circling and joining with a line. Together, discuss what is common about all these words (they share the same ending le).
- Show Me: On dry-wipe boards, children spell a few more words, concentrating on getting the ending correct, e.g. trickle, candle, uncle.
- Ask the children to make up a few nonsense sentences, using a different colour to distinguish the le, e.g.
  *The little pickle had a chuckle in the middle of an apple.*
  *The simple dimple was able to lay the table.*
- Introduce the oddbod: *they* – see below.

**Pupil activities**

A:  Sort into double letters plus le; ckle; dle.
B:  Sort into two patterns: ible; ble.
C:  Sort into three patterns: ble, ple; cle.

Extra challenge: Find and list exceptions spelt al or el, e.g. *pedal*, *parcel*.

**Review**

- What is the most common ending for a word that ends in the sound l? (le as in middle.)

**Homework**  Funny poem cloze procedure.

---

**Oddbod**   they  ⌒

- They – how can we remember this?
- Use rhyme: *They don't eat hay.*
- Use words in words: Is it he, the or they?
- Splitting up: The plus y.

**Snip-snap**   Quickfire Rhymes  ✍

- Say a word ending in le. Children write down a rhyme for it, e.g. *table* (*able*), *pickle* (*tickle*), *wriggle* (*giggle*), *fumble* (*tumble*).
- Help strugglers by giving a first sound clue, e.g. *trouble* (d).

**NLS objective for Unit 3**

3.1.W9 (See Spelling Bank page 5)

**Part 2** | **You need**   Big Book page 7; two different-coloured pens; dry-wipe boards or notebooks in pairs

**Whole class**
- Recap – spelling words that end in le.
- Look at the BBk page. Investigate what happens when ly, ed or ing endings are added to words that end in le (see Review).
- Fill in the table together asking the children to suggest spellings. Focus on the double consonants in *giggle* and *cuddle*. Remind children that a short vowel sound like the **i** and **u** in these words is always followed by a double consonant when we add an ending like le.
- Invite children to add other words to the chart.
- Time Out/Show Me: Children work in pairs to write completed words.
- Check spelling visually – does it look right?
- Ask children to complete the following sentence: 'When you add an ly, ed or ing to a word that ends in le, you ...'.

**Review**
- Words that end in the **l** sound and are spelt le drop the e when adding ed or ing, and drop le when adding ly.

- Homework review.
- Perform the homework rhyme (from PCM 3) as a class.
- In pairs, the children double-check for correct spelling of endings of rhyming words – did anyone get caught out?

**Follow-up homework**
- Children make a note of the most common le words and check that they spell them correctly, e.g. *little, middle, bicycle*.

**Test dictation**
OB They put the hot food on the plate.
A    My sister and I love to giggle. Wednesday is in the middle of the week.
B    Bob got on his bicycle and went away. The work we did today was simple.
C    The boys and girls were being very sensible.

---

**Snip-snap**   Adding ly
- Dictation onto dry-wipe boards – 'Add ly to these words: *prickle, tickle, able, reliable*.'
- Ask: What did you do? What's the rule?

**Snip-snap**   Who-hoo
- Write down 'hoo' (say 'hoooo' to exaggerate).
- Now write 'whoo' – point out silent w.
- A way of remembering is 'silent w, disappearing o' – write up 'who'.
- Children practise writing 'who' swiftly on dry-wipe boards.

# 4 Common prefixes

## Part 1 | You need

Big Book page 8; different-coloured pens; dry-wipe boards or notebooks in pairs; Pupil's Book pages 8–9; PCM 4

**Whole class**

- Introduce the objective: adding prefixes to words. (Note that not all words which have prefixes in the strict sense produce free-standing word roots when the prefixes are removed, e.g. *exit, present*.)
- Look at the BBk page and read through the text as it stands.
- Alter together, by adding either un or re, using different-coloured pens. Add in the incidental point about using *an* before a vowel. (Note that some words, especially where the prefix ends in a vowel and the word root starts with a vowel, may use hyphens.)
- Children suggest which would work by thumbs up or down. Discuss how the changes alter the meanings (un means 'not' or '(doing) the opposite of' and re means 'again').
- Time Out/Show Me: Ask children to make up sentences on dry-wipe boards using a word containing a prefix, e.g. un*tidy*, un*seen*, re*play*, re*place*.
- Discuss meanings of de ('away from' or '(doing) the opposite of'), dis ('not' or 'the opposite of') and pre ('before' or 'in advance') on the basis of any words that can be thought up.
- Introduce the oddbods: *are, our* – see below.

**Pupil activities**

A: Change meanings of some sentences by adding a prefix (un or re).
B: Sort words by prefix (de and un).
C: Sort words by prefix (re, dis and pre).

Think about …: Whether words have prefixes.

**Review**

- How do the prefixes un and re change the meaning of words?

**Homework**

Sort and find words with prefixes re and un, then write some sentences.

---

**Oddbods**   are, our 😊 🎵
- Say the words carefully and listen to the difference.
- Write up *our* and *are*. Say them, over-emphasising the difference: 'Arrr', 'Owrrr'.
- Make up short phrases with both words, e.g. 'Are you coming to our place?'

**Snip-snap**   Play 'Beat the Clock' ✍
- Give a fixed time limit to write down words that share one prefix, e.g. un, re, dis, pre, de (un*tie*, un*do*, un*tidy*, un*happy*).

**NLS objectives for Unit 4**

3.1.W10      3.1.W12 (See Spelling Bank page 6)

## Part 2 | You need      Big Book page 9; coloured pens; dry-wipe boards or notebooks in pairs

**Whole class**
- Revise what was learnt in the previous session – how the prefixes un and re alter the meanings of words (un means 'not' or '(doing) the opposite of' and re means 'again').
- Look at the BBk page, reading the text through and looking at the illustrations.
- Cross out or alter the prefixes of the underlined words.
- Ask the children how this changes the meanings.
- Compose some sentences together using prefixes (e.g. *My room is* un*tidy sometimes, when I* un*pack my toys, but when my mum reminds me, I remain tidy*.)

**Review**
- How do the prefixes un and re change the meaning of words?
- Homework review.
- Can you remember what the prefixes mean?

**Follow-up homework**
- Children flick through their writing book or a piece of their own writing, and make a list of the words they use most that contain a prefix.

**Test dictation**
OB   Our school is in the middle of town and we are happy there.
A     Unclean hands need soap and water. I feel unwell in a boat.
B     Dad predicted that Sue would win. The amazing car disappeared down the road.
C     John put his head underneath the water.

---

**Snip-snap**   Find the Prefix
- Write up the five prefixes un, de, dis, re, pre.
- You say a word, e.g. turn, fix, please, fuse, zip.
- The children respond by jotting down a relevant prefix.

**Snip-snap**   Joining Up
- Practise writing 'they are' and 'we are'.
- Use joined writing.

# Making opposites

---

**Objective for Unit 5**

To use prefixes to make new words

---

**Part 1** | **You need**    Big Book page 10; coloured pens; Pupil's Book pages 10–11; PCM 5

**Whole class**
- Introduce the objective: using prefixes to make opposites.
- Revisit what can be remembered from the previous unit (prefixes).
- Look at the BBk page and read text together, then find matching pairs, e.g. *happy/unhappy*.
- Ask the children which prefixes are used. How do they change the meanings of the words? (un means 'not' or '(doing) the opposite of'; dis means 'not' or 'the opposite of')
- Together, list on the board other words that can be changed into their opposites by adding or altering a prefix.
- Get up and Go: individuals write up their suggestions.
- Then make up and write a few sentences, using different colours to distinguish the prefixes, e.g.
    *He smiled happily and she cried unhappily.*
    *It was an unpleasant story, so it was pleasant to stop reading.*
    *Disconnect the phone and connect the computer instead.*
- Introduce the oddbod: *moment* – see below.

**Pupil activities**
A:    Create opposites using un or dis.
B:    Rewrite the letter so that Tom and Sam have a good time.
C:    Separate prefixes from their roots.

Extra challenge: Collect words that start with anti.

**Review**
- How do prefixes such as un or dis change the meaning of words? (They create opposites.)

**Homework**
Rewrite the school report by removing/adding prefixes to show Mo in a better light!

---

**Oddbod**    moment  ✍ ☺
- Emphasise the syllables 'mo/ment'.
- 'Mo' is easy – mo.
- So is 'ment' – just as it is said m-e-n with t on the end.

**Snip-snap**    'Beat the Clock' Again  ✎
- Use an appropriate time limit for your class.
- Write on dry-wipe boards the opposites of the following words: *able, zip, kind, trust, tie, obey.*
- Which prefixes helped? (un, dis)

**NLS objectives for Unit 5**

3.1.W11 (See Spelling Bank page 7)     3.1.W12

## Part 2 | **You need**     Big Book page 11; coloured pens; dry-wipe boards or notebooks in pairs

**Whole class**
- Recap on the previous session.
- Look at the BBk page and read through the secret message.
- Rewrite the relevant words together, dropping or altering the prefixes, to change the message and put the crooks on the wrong track:
  (*disobey/obey*; *anti-clockwise/clockwise*; *discontinue/continue*; *impossible/possible*; *invisible/visible*; *disconnect/connect*; *decrease/increase*; *explode/implode*; *unfasten/fasten*; *outside/inside*; *unlock/lock*).

**Review**
- Summarise: many words can be made opposite in meaning by using a prefix such as un, dis, non, anti, de, mis, im, ir, il or in.
  Knowing this helps with spelling.

- Homework review.
- Share a version of Mo's amended school report. Focus on prefixes used.

**Follow-up homework**
- Children write a good school report about a friend, using lots of words with prefixes.

**Test dictation**
- OB  I will help you in a moment.
- A  Ben disliked diving into the water. You must not disobey Mum and Dad.
- B  Unfortunately I was unwell at the weekend. The unpleasant food sat on my plate.
- C  The homework we had was impossible.

---

**Snip-snap**  Finding Roots
- Say a word that includes a prefix, e.g. *dislike*.
  The children say the word root, e.g. *like*.
- Possible words – *nonsense, misbehave, impossible, disobey, disagree, untidy, undo, unkind*.

**Snip-snap**  Quick Write
- On dry-wipe boards, rapidly write down 'after', joining the letters, five times.
- Remind the children – there are no words that are spelt arf, except in comics when a dog barks or someone laughs!

# 6 Spelling strategies

**Objective for Unit 6**

To use a range of strategies

## Part 1

**You need**  Big Book page 12; coloured pens; dry-wipe boards or notebooks in pairs; Pupil's Book pages 12–13; PCM 6

**Whole class**
- Introduce the objective: different strategies for spelling.
- Start a checklist: 'If we get stuck on a word we can ...' e.g. use sounds, letter patterns, rhyme.
- Look at the BBk page and use the basic pattern to play 'Shannon's Game' – which is like 'Hangman' but the letters must be guessed in the right order.
- Decide on a word (e.g. *grey*) and draw four lines in the boxes at the bottom of the page. Give the children the first letter and focus on 'serial probability', i.e. what is most likely to come next/what cannot come next?
- t is not possible; r might be a contender (*grab*) or e (*gets*). Ask the children to take it in turns to guess the second letter. Once someone guesses r, write it over the second line. If they guess incorrectly, begin to draw over the hangman shape, one bit at a time.
- If a child wants to try guessing the word, invite them to come up and scribe their suggestion in the box.
- Keep going until they have completed the word or the man is hanged.
- Once the children are familiar with the game, it can be extended so that they also guess the first letter of the word.
- Introduce the oddbod: *out* – see below.

**Pupil activities**
- A:  Work in pairs to build word 'towers' starting from a single letter.
- B:  Make words from the letters of another word.
- C:  Cloze procedure.

Think about ...: Different spelling strategies to double-check the spellings of words.

**Review**
- Add to the list of spelling strategies – using what we know about which letters are likely or unlikely to follow each other.

**Homework**  Inventing own mnemonics and spelling tricks.

---

**Oddbod**  out ☺ ☺
- Say the word slowly, emphasising the two sounds – **owwww/ttt**.
- Write it up showing the two parts ou – t.
- One easy way to remember the spelling is that you shout out!

**Snip-snap**  Seeing It ☺
- Play 'Right or Wrong' – emphasis on 'does it look right?'
- You write up a word, spelt in several different ways (e.g. write up: *becos, becuse, because*).
- Children put thumbs up or down OR write on dry-wipe boards the version they think is correct.
- Ask: 'Which one is it? How do you know?'

---

**NLS objective for Unit 6**

3.1.W6

---

**Part 2** | **You need**  Big Book page 13; coloured pens; dry-wipe boards in pairs

**Whole class**
- Look back at the checklist of spelling strategies begun in Part 1.
- Look at the BBk page and read through the text, pausing at the gaps where words are missing.
- Together, use a range of strategies, double-checking with other strategies, and supply the missing words:
  *people, little, many, know, they, eight, their, many, poison, claws, grabbing, grow, dry, around.*
- Try out spellings on the board, then check to see if they 'look right'. Model some words and use Get Up and Go: Children spell out their guesses. Discuss strategies used.

**Review**
- Complete the list of possible strategies, e.g.
  - sounding out
  - does it look right?
  - does it have a common pattern?
  - are there other words that start or end in the same way?
  - are there other words related by meaning?
  - are there words that rhyme?
  - is there a rule or pattern?
  - do I have a way of remembering this?
- Homework review.
- Share any useful mnemonics or spelling tricks that children have found.

**Follow-up homework**
- Children make a note of useful mnemonics that they will want to use, especially for common words.

**Test dictation**
OB  We went out in the boat together.
A   The new boy did not disobey Mrs Green. Her boat has a tall mast.
B   At night the moon comes out. The men predicted another wet Friday.
C   You should eat lots of vegetables every day.

---

**Snip-snap**   Writing It
- Write up a NLS key word in the top left-hand corner of the board. Try: *people, half, again.*
- The children to look up and to the left; say the word and repeat it, slowly, bit by bit; then they write the word, rewriting over the top several times to 'get the feel'.
- Ask them to 'take a picture' – remember what it looks like.

**Snip-snap**   Hearing It
- Emphasis on 'hear it' – use of phonics.
- Pretending to be robots, children sound out words as a class, e.g. *vest, shed, test, deck, stamp, had, train, book, shirt, bowl, moon, soap, peach, pound, sweets, crown, corner, crumb,* etc.

# Vowel phonemes or, er and air

**Objective for Unit 7**

Revision of **or**, **er**, **air** phonemes and letter patterns

## Part 1

**You need**  Big Book page 14; two different-coloured pens; dry-wipe boards or notebooks in pairs; Pupil's Book pages 14–15; PCM 7

**Whole class**
- Introduce the objective: looking at different ways of spelling the **or** and **er** phonemes.
- Look at the BBk page and read through the poem together, then ask the children to suggest which words have **or** and **er** phonemes.
- Underline these in different colours to distinguish. (Some of this work varies, depending on regional accent.)
- List the possible spelling alternatives, e.g.
  **or** = or (p*or*t), oor (*floor*), aw (cl*aw*), au (c*augh*t), ore (st*ore*)
  **er** = er (h*er*), ir (b*ir*d), ur (f*ur*), or (w*or*d), ear (h*ear*d).
  These could be listed on a large sheet of paper and kept for future use.
  The children could note them in their spelling logs.
- Together, compose nonsense sentences, using the two vowel phonemes, e.g.
  *The st**or**k's cl**aw** got c**augh**t in the p**or**thole.*
  *The silly b**ir**d had no w**or**d to say since it st**ir**red.*
- Introduce the oddbod: *girl* – see below.

**Pupil activities**
- A:  Find five **or** words and five **er** words in sentences.
- B:  Find **or** and **er** words in a pyramid.
- C:  Sort out **or**, **er** and **air** words, plus those that rhyme.

Extra challenge: Find the most common spelling of words with the **er** phoneme.

**Review**
- The vowel phonemes **or** and **er** can be spelt in different ways.

**Homework**
The vowel phonemes **or** and **er** can be spelt in different ways.

**Homework**
Investigating likely spellings of **or** words. (Note that children's responses to this exercise may vary according to their accent.)

---

**Oddbod**  girl  👁 😄
- Look at the word. Which is the bit that causes a problem? Underline it.
- The most common error is to write *gril* – but if you blend this, it reads 'grill'. That cannot be right.
- Segment *girl* = **g**-**ir**-**l**.

**Snip-snap**  Thumbs Up, Thumbs Down  🕐
- Say a word containing the phoneme **or** or **er**.
- Children listen carefully and put thumbs up if it contains **or** and down if it contains **er**.
- Throw in the odd one that contains neither sound. Try mixing up the following:
  **er** = *her, were, bird, heard, surf, burnt, learn, girl, twirl, world.*
  **or** = *sport, caught, thought, floor, door, paw, claw, for, more.*

| | |
|---|---|
| **NLS objective for Unit 7** | |
| 3.2.W1 | |

## Part 2 | You need    Big Book page 15; coloured pens; dry-wipe boards or notebooks in pairs

**Whole class**
- Recap different ways of spelling **or** and **er** phonemes.
- Look at the BBk page and read through the passage, then ask children to suggest which words have the **air** phoneme. (Some of this work varies, depending on regional accent.)
- Underline in a colour to distinguish.
- List the possible spelling alternatives for **air** words, e.g.
  air (*flair*), are (*rare*), ere (*there*), ear (*wear*).
- Together, compose sentences using the **air** phoneme, e.g.
  *There was a rabbit caught in a snare.*
  *The bear decided to wear a pair of flared trousers.*

**Review**
- The vowel phoneme **air** can be spelt in different ways, e.g.
  air (*fair*), are (*dare*), ere (*there*), ear (*pear*).
- Homework review.
- Which is the most likely spelling of the **air** phoneme?

**Follow-up homework**
- Children make a note of any other common words built around the **er**, **air** and **or** phonemes, e.g.
  *taught, thought, before, scary*, etc.

**Test dictation**
- OB  The little girl was talking nonsense.
- A  My brother was born in October. Jen loves to play sport.
- B  I taught Tim to throw a ball. Do not put food on the dirty plate.
- C  The unpleasant boy would not share his ice-cream.

---

**Snip-snap**    Listening Game
- Say a word containing the phoneme **or**, **er** or **air**.
- Children listen carefully and put thumbs up if it contains **or**, down if it contains **er**, and hand in the air for **air**.
- Throw in the odd one that contains none of the sounds. Try mixing up:
  **air** = *fair, bear, lair, pare, square, share, there, Blair, stare, chair.*
  **er** = *her, were, bird, heard, for, turf, learn, girl, whirl, world, pearl.*
  **or** = *sport, taught, caught, short, floor, door, paw, claw, for, shore, raw, broad.*

**Snip-snap**    Rhyming
- Write up a word (use the same bank of words as in previous Snip-snap). Children call out a rhyme.
- They score a point for each correct rhyme. Two points for a word with the same sound, but a different spelling (e.g. *door, claw*).

# Adding <u>er</u>, <u>est</u> and y

---

### Objective for Unit 8

To investigate what happens when er, est and y are added to words

---

## Part 1 | You need

Big Book page 16; three different-coloured pens; dry-wipe boards or notebooks in pairs; Pupil's Book pages 16–17; PCM 8

**Whole class**

- Introduce the first part of the objective: adding er and est to words.
- Look at the BBk page and ask the children why they have been written in the way they have. (To show what the words mean and how they change.)
- Ask: 'What patterns can you see?' Underline the base word in one colour, er in another colour and est in yet another, and point out the three ways of adding er or est:
  - typical words – just add er or est;
  - 'short' vowels – words with 'short' vowels just before the final consonant, double the consonant;
  - y words – words ending in y change the y to i.
- There are also catch-you-outs where the word changes completely, e.g. *good – better – best*.
- Write a few sentences using some of the words, e.g.
  *The smallest mouse was chased by the fattest cat.*
  *The chillier the day grew, the longer the icicles became.*
- Introduce the oddbod: *first* – see below.

**Pupil activities**

A:  Draw calligrams.
B:  Write boastful replies.
C:  Write est sentences.

Extra challenge: Find irregular words and words that use *more* and *most*.

**Review**

- Recap the four ways of adding er and est.
- Remind children of another way of adding er or est: words that end in e drop the e and then add the ending.

**Homework**

Adding er and est to words and noting spelling rules.

---

**Oddbod**   first  😑 👁

- Draw children's attention to the **ir** sound.
- Ask them to suggest other words with that sound.
- Discuss different ways of spelling the sound (e.g. ur, or, er, ear).
- Ask who knows what comes after *first* and practise spelling *second*, *third*, etc.

**Snip-snap**   Big, Bigger, Biggest  ✍

- Focus on common words, e.g. you write up *cold*.
- Children write down *colder, coldest*.
- Try using *tall, quick, high*.

**NLS objectives for Unit 8**

3.2.W8 (See Spelling Bank pages 8–9)

**Part 2** | **You need**  Big Book page 17; three different-coloured pens; dry-wipe boards or notebooks in pairs

**Whole class**
- Introduce the second part of the objective: adding y to words.
- Look at the BBk page and sort the words using the three columns:
  - typical words – just add y;
  - e words – words that end in e drop the e and then add the ending;
  - 'short' vowels – words with 'short' vowels just before the final consonant, double the consonant.
- There are catch-you-outs – *holey*, where the e is not dropped so that you can distinguish it from *holy* (which is not a word commonly applied to socks!); and *dyeing* (to distinguish it from *dying*). Also, words like *blurry* double the final consonant even though they don't have a 'short' vowel phoneme.

**Review**
- Recap the three ways of adding y.

- Homework review.
- Use what you now know about these words to help you spell.

**Follow-up homework**
- Children make a note of what they have learnt about er, est and y. They should look out for these word endings – especially in Maths.

**Test dictation**
OB  I will be first at school today.
A    My bicycle is bigger than yours.
     June is hotter than January.
B    It is quickest to go by car.
     We are getting closer and closer.
C    Jess is the craziest girl in our school.

---

**Snip-snap**   Even Bigger
- Focus on words with 'short' vowels. You write up *big*.
- Children add er, est and write down *bigger*, *biggest*.
- Try using *hot, thin, fat*.

**Snip-snap**   Adding y
- Focus on words that add y. You write up *mist*.
- Children add y and write down *misty*.
- Try using *paper, blur, haze*.

# 9 Spelling plurals

## Part 1

**You need** Big Book page 18; coloured pens; dry-wipe boards or notebooks in pairs; Pupil's Book pages 18–19; PCM 9

**Whole class**
- Introduce the objectives: spelling plurals, and using the terms *singular* and *plural*.
- Focus on the BBk page and read the passage through, underlining all the plurals.
- Let the children sort these out into two columns – words which just add s and words which add es.
- Ask the children to think of a rule for the es column. (The rule is that you add es if the word ends in a hissing/buzzing/shushing sound, generally words that end in s, x, z, ch or sh. Another way to remember this is to add on es if you can hear an extra syllable when you say the plural form.)
- Write a few sentences using plurals, e.g.
  *The cats ran away from the foxes.*
  *The ducks swam on the ponds.*
  *The girls wore their hair in bunches.*
  and together, change the plurals to singulars.
- Introduce the oddbod: *last* – see below.

**Pupil activities**
- A: Sorting plurals.
- B: Changing plurals to singular and vice versa.
- C: Inventing a number rhyme.

Extra challenge: Finding irregular plurals, with the help of dictionaries.

**Review**
- What happens to most nouns when they become plural? They add s.
- Those that end with a shushing/hissing/buzzing sound add es.

**Homework** Investigation of plurals of words that end in o.

---

**Oddbod** last 👁
- You write up *larst* and *last*.
- Ask the children which looks right.
- Children list other words that are said and written using the same letter pattern, e.g. *last, fast, cast, mast, past, plaster, faster, aghast, blast, vast, flabbergast, forecast, outlast, contrast, downcast.*

**Snip-snap** Quickfire Plurals 🔊
- You write up a singular word and the children have to quickly say the plural.
- Begin with common words that end in s, e.g. *dog, cat, cup, pen, day, tick, crack, age, pond, bramble, game.*

18

---

**NLS objectives for Unit 9**

3.2.W9    3.2.W11 (See Spelling Bank page 10)

---

**Part 2** | **You need**    Big Book page 19; coloured pens; dry-wipe boards or notebooks in pairs

**Whole class**
- Revise what was learned in the previous session.
- Focus on the BBk page and sort the words into columns. Tell the children the rules:
    - Most words just add s (*dogs*).
    - Shushing/hissing/buzzing words add es (*foxes*)
    - Words that end in y change the y to i and add es (*babies*), unless the final letter is preceded by a vowel (*days*).
    - Some words that end in f or fe change the f to v and add es (*elves, calves, thieves*); others merely add s, e.g. *roofs, chiefs, beliefs*.
- There are a few catch-you-outs where many dictionaries now give acceptable alternatives, such as *hoofs/hooves*.

**Review**
- Recap on the four-part rule for making plurals.

- Homework review.
- Think of words that end in o but just add s not es.

**Follow-up homework**
- Make a checklist in your spelling log of what you have learned from the homework and previous sessions about making plurals.

**Test dictation**
OB  Tom was slipping into last place.
A    The cats lay underneath the bushes.
     You should not play with matches.
B    The crying babies were very noisy.
     We were disappointed not to see the foxes.
C    The thieves took my new red bicycle.

---

**Snip-snap**    Plural Practice
- Focus on words that end in s, x, z, ch and sh, as these generally add es. Mix in words that just add s.
- You write up the singulars, e.g. *hutch, pit, bus, tune, princess, boss, band, patch, gun, fish.*
- Children alter these to plurals.

**Snip-snap**    Perfect Your Plurals
- Focus on words ending in y that have a consonant before the y. These change the y to ies, e.g. *baby – babies*. Mix in words that just add s.
- You write up the singulars, e.g. *bin, nappy, train, party, plane, difficulty, plant, ferry, hat, berry.*
- Children alter these to plurals.

# Compound words and apostrophes

---

**Objectives for Unit 10**

To spell compound words; to use the contraction apostrophe

---

**Part 1** | **You need** — Big Book page 20; coloured pens; dry-wipe boards or notebooks in pairs; Pupil's Book pages 20–21; PCM 10

**Whole class**
- Introduce the first objective: spelling compound words.
- Look at the BBk page and read out the words – tell the class they are called 'compound' words.
- Ask the children: Looking at the way the words are made, what do you think 'compound' means?
- Add other examples that children can think of, built around the words in the table, e.g. *lunchtime, goldfish, eyebrow.*
- Write a few (sensible or nonsense) sentences using compound words, e.g.
  *The cowboy walked upstairs.*
  *The earthworm slept in the dustbin.*
  *On Sunday the goalkeeper fed his sheepdog at dinnertime.*
- Introduce the oddbod: *clue* – see below.

**Pupil activities**
A: Make compound words.
B: Make compound words.
C: Break up compound words and write sentences.

Extra challenge: Invent compound words.

**Review**
- Compounds are usually nouns and are made by joining two or more smaller words. They are easy to spell if you know how to spell the smaller words.

**Homework** — Making compound words.

---

**Oddbod**   clue 👁 👄 👂 💭
- Write up *clue/clew/clo/cloo* – ask the children which 'looks right'.
- Chant the letters rhythmically – 'c-l-u-e'.
- Rhymes with *true, blue, glue* and *due.*
- Who can invent a mnemonic? (e.g. *children like ugly elephants*)

**Snip-snap**   Compound Words 👂✍
- You say a word, e.g. *fruit.*
- Children write down compound words such as *fruitcake, passion-fruit, grapefruit.*
- Try: *ear, sand, air, over, handed, power.*

---

**NLS objectives for Unit 10**

3.2.W12     3.2.W15 (See Spelling Bank pages 12 and 15)

---

**Part 2** | **You need**     Big Book page 21; coloured pens; dry-wipe boards or notebooks in pairs

**Whole class**
- Introduce the second objective: using apostrophes to spell short forms of words.
- To avoid apostrophes being scattered like confetti, restrict children to using them only for omission at this stage (i.e., not for possessives).
- Look at the BBk page and pair up the words, joining the monster to its correct hat, e.g. *do not – don't*.
- Discuss the missing letter(s). There is a catch-you-out in *won't*, which also introduces a letter that was not there originally. Also mention that the short forms are written as one word, without spaces.
- Together, discuss when shortened forms are used like this in writing – in direct speech and less formal writing.
- Write a few pieces of dialogue using apostrophes, e.g.
  *"I can't and I won't," said Tom.*
  *"Well, don't then – it won't help anyway," Jerry replied.*

**Review**
- Summarise what is known about apostrophes for omission – they replace letters, shorten the word and are often used in dialogue.
- Homework review.
- Some compound words are joined by hyphens (e.g. *king-sized*) or are made of two words used together but with a space between (e.g. *ski lift*). See how many you can find.

**Follow-up homework**
- Children make a note of words with apostrophes that they use most often in their own writing.

**Test dictation**
OB  Can you give me a clue?
A    Does anybody dislike pancakes?
       Nobody enjoys trouble.
B    I had pancakes for breakfast today.
       Sam put the plates in the cupboard.
C    I'm going to be nine on Thursday.

---

**Snip-snap**     Make It Informal ... ②
- You say a phrase.
- Children make it informal by using an apostrophe, e.g. *will not – won't*.
- Try using *I am, I will, I had, you are, I have, he will, here is, is not, would not*.

**Snip-snap**     ... And Formal Again  ② ✍
- You say a word using an apostrophe for omission.
- Children write out the full form, e.g. *don't – do not*.
- Try using: *they're, won't, doesn't, can't, I've, it's*.

### Objectives for Unit 11

To investigate silent letters; contraction apostrophes

## Part 1

**You need**  Big Book page 22; coloured pens; dry-wipe boards or notebooks in pairs; Pupil's Book pages 22–23; PCM 11

**Whole class**
- Introduce the first objective: spelling words with silent letters.
- Look at the BBk page and ask the children to listen as you read the passage. Pronounce the silent letters as you read.
- Let the children join in. Underline the silent letters as you read. Discuss how, years ago, some 'silent' letters were actually pronounced. One way to remember these spellings is to over-pronounce the silent letter, e.g. **k**/*now*.
- Sort the words with silent letters into two types (gn and kn). Ask the children: what can you work out about the two patterns? (Both kn and gn start the word and are followed by a vowel.)
- List any other examples the children know.
- Together, write a few sentences using words with silent letters, e.g.

   *To write on your wrist is wrong.*
   *Let's wrestle with a wrapper.*
   *Can you find a rhyme for 'rhubarb'?*
   *When the whale whines, the rhino should not doubt.*
   *The honest chemist wrestled with the wretched lamb and bit his dumb thumb.*

- Note – some children will pronounce the wh words with an aspirated w, that is, pronouncing the h.
- Introduce the oddbod: *answer* – see below.

**Pupil activities**
A:   Read a passage, list and sort words with silent letters (gn and kn).
B:   Insert missing silent letters.
C:   Read a passage, list and sort words with silent letters (w, h, b, k, l).

Extra challenge: Write a story using words with silent letters.

**Review**
- Some words have silent letters. One way to remember them is to over-pronounce the silent letter, e.g. *island* = **is**/*land*.

**Homework**   Crossword that hinges on silent letters.

---

**Oddbod**   answer
- Say the word as it is written, over-pronouncing the letters, 'an-sswer'.
- Note that the start is easy, ans, and that we comes next, then just add r.
- Children write the word on dry-wipe boards. Remind them that there is a we in answer.

**Snip-snap**   Shhh Letters
- Practise joined writing of kn and gn – quickly.
- Segment words like a robot and write on dry-wipe boards, words that use these silent letters.
- Try: *knee, knit, knock, knot, kneel, gnat, gnash.*

---

**NLS objectives for Unit 11**

3.2.W10      3.2.W15 (See Spelling Bank pages 11 and 15)

---

**Part 2** | **You need**      Big Book page 23; coloured pens; dry-wipe boards or notebooks in pairs

**Whole class**
- Revise what was learnt in the previous unit on apostrophes for missing letters, e.g. *couldn't = could not*.
- Look at the BBk page and read the passage together. Re-read using a narrator and two characters.
- Underline the words that have apostrophes.
- Ask the children whether this dialogue sounds formal or informal. How do they know?
- Now change the relationship between the characters. Cross out and rewrite the contractions as full forms, making the dialogue sound more formal.
- Show Me: Children help by writing full forms on dry-wipe boards.
- Re-read and discuss how this alters the tone.
- Write a short sequence of dialogue, focusing on contractions: e.g.
  *"Aren't you coming swimming?"*
  *"No. I'd like to, but I can't."*

**Review**
- Recap on the situations where apostrophes are commonly used, i.e. informal direct speech and informal writing.

- Homework review.
- Make a checklist of what has been learnt about words with silent letters.
- Summarise what is known about apostrophes and missing letters.

**Follow-up homework**
- Children make a note of words that they often use that have silent letters and ways to remember them, e.g. *island = **is**/land*.

**Test dictation**
- OB  Liz got up to answer the telephone.
- A    There was a loud knock at the door.
       I know Bob did something bad.
- B    I'm going to write to my sister.
       I honestly can't tell you the answer.
- C    She's going to the fair, but it doesn't matter.

---

**Snip-snap**    Make It Informal …  
- You say a phrase.
- Children make it informal by using apostrophe for missing letter(s), e.g. *will not – won't*.
- Try using *here is, it is, we are, will not, could not, will not, you are, did not*.

**Snip-snap**    … And Formal Again  
- You say a word using an apostrophe for missing letter(s).
- Children say the full form, e.g. *don't – do not*.
- Try using *what's, he's, it's, they're, he'll, wouldn't, won't, I've*.

# 12 Common suffixes

## Part 1 | You need

Big Book page 24; coloured pens; dry-wipe boards or notebooks in pairs; Pupil's Book pages 24–25; PCM 12

**Whole class**

- Introduce the objectives: spelling suffixes – bits that go at the end of words like ly, ful and less – and using them to generate new words.
- Look at the BBk page and together, match the suffix to the base word, e.g. *wish*/ful.
- Time Out/Show Me: Children make other combinations on dry-wipe boards.
- Draw attention to any where spelling of the base word alters, e.g. *funnily*/*pitiful* are examples of the y changing to i.
- Discuss how the suffix ful has only one l (though becomes fully if you add ly on, e.g. *wonder*ful – *wonder*fully).
- Use the bottom of the page for composing sentences together, using words from each group, e.g.
  *The kindly teacher was both fearless and hopeful.*
- Introduce the oddbod: *lovely* – see below.

**Pupil activities**

- A: Add the right suffix to words in sentences (note that the last two sentences have alternatives, e.g. *fearful* or *fearless*; *careful* or *careless*).
- B: Add the right suffix to words in a passage.
- C: Create extra lines for a poem, using suffixes (judge whether children will need to refer to the words on the BBk pages).

Extra challenge: Write a poem following a pattern, using words with suffixes.

**Review**

- Suffixes are attached to base words to make different meanings: less means 'without' or 'having no'; ly means 'in this way'; and ful means 'the amount that can be held by' or 'full of'.

**Homework**

Writing sentences using words ending in er, ful and less.

---

**Oddbod**   lovely  ②⌣☺
- Ask who can tell you what type of word *love* is? (noun) What type of word does it become when we add ly? (adjective)
- Chant the letters 'l-o-v-e-l-y' and the phrase 'lovely lollipops'.

**Snip-snap**   Change the Gender ✎⌣
- You write up these words: *princess, huntress, waitress, headmistress, hostess, duchess, lioness.*
- What do pupils think *ess* means? ('female')
- Get children to jot down masculine forms, e.g. *prince, hunter,* etc. Watch out for the *headmister*!

---

**NLS objectives for Unit 12**

3.2.W13    3.2.W14 (See Spelling Bank pages 13–14)

---

## Part 2 | You need    Big Book page 25; coloured pens; dry-wipe boards or notebooks in pairs

**Whole class**
- Revise what was learnt in the previous session.
- Look at the BBk page and together, make some word sums by putting base words together with a suffix.
- Focus on one base word at a time, e.g. *cheer*.
- Children make words on their dry-wipe boards – try 'proper' words (*cheerful*, *cheerless*) and 'invented' words (*cheerer*, *cheerable*). Make sure they know which are which!
- Together, create sentences at the bottom of the page, using 'proper' words and trying where possible to illuminate the meaning of each suffix by the context.
- Note how occasionally a base word ending in e has to drop the e, e.g. *lone* + er becomes *loner*.

**Review**
- Recap the four ways that suffixes can be added to base words: just add; drop e and then add; double the final consonant before a 'short' vowel and then add; change y to i and then add.

- Homework review.
- Did anyone use all the words in the 'word pools'?

**Follow-up homework**
- Children find words that have two suffixes. What (if anything) happens to the spelling of the first suffix when the second one is added?
  They should compare, e.g. *gracefully* (*grace* + ful + ly), *funnily* (*fun* + double consonant n + change y to i before adding ly).

**Test dictation**
- OB  People need a lovely breakfast.
- A   The fearless girl played with the bear.
     I would like Saturday to be endless.
- B   I would like to write a successful book.
     Nobody is as friendly as Joe.
- C   You become a teenager at thirteen.

---

**Snip-snap**   Quickfire Oddbod
- Remember *many* is linked to *any* – they both have to do with numbers of things or people.
- Children write *many* on dry-wipe boards, joining up the letters.
- Who can write the word five times in 30 seconds?

**Snip-snap**   Beat the Clock
- In one minute, see who can think of and write down the most words that end in a suffix, e.g. wards (*downwards*, *backwards*, *upwards*). You could also try ed, ing, ous, ment, ance, hood. Try to work out what each suffix means or does.

<table>
<tr><td colspan="2">Objective for Unit 13<br>Revision of phonemes and spelling strategies</td></tr>
</table>

## Part 1

**You need** Big Book page 26; coloured pens; dry-wipe boards or notebooks in pairs; Pupil's Book pages 26–27; PCM 13

**Whole class**

- Introduce the objective: using segmentation as a basic spelling strategy and exploring the vowel phonemes **ai** and **oy**.
- Look at the BBk page and read the passage, stopping at those words which are underlined.
- Together, break the underlined words into syllables (e.g. *a-way*). Then take each syllable and separate each sound (**a-w-a-y**). (Note that the passage can be revisited later for more sounding-out work.)
- Now underline words with the phoneme **ai** in one colour and words with the phoneme **oy** in another.
- List the words in five columns, differentiated by spelling. (The letter combinations ai, ay, a-e, oi and oy occur in these words.)
- Ask children to work in pairs to identify where the vowels come in the words in each column. (Writing the vowels in different colours can help some children see the pattern more clearly.)
- Establish that, often, ay and oy will come at the end of the words and ai and oi in the middle.
- Compose sentences together, splitting longer words into syllables, then segmenting each syllable, listening to the sounds. For example:
  *I get no enjoyment from reading about royalty; We went sailing in the daytime; Begin by boiling the carrots in a large container.*
- Introduce the oddbod: *help* – see below.

**Pupil activities**

A: Spell words with the letter patterns oi or oy.
B: Spell words with the letter patterns oi, oy, ai or ay.
C: Alternative spellings of the 'long' vowel phoneme **ai**.

Extra challenge: Wordsearch, finding words with the **oy** and **ai** phonemes.

**Review**
- Recap what has been learnt – letter patterns ay and oy tend to appear at the ends of words; ai and oi tend to appear in the middle of words.

**Homework**
Counting syllables and looking for words within words.

---

**Oddbod** help 😵 👁 💬
- Segment slowly and carefully to hear each sound in order – '**h-e-l-p**'.
- Learn by 'looking' – visualise the word.
- Learn by chanting the letters 'h-e-l-p'.
- Mnemonics – '*h*eroes *e*nter *l*onely *p*laces'; or '*h*elp *e*very *l*ost *p*erson'.

**Snip-snap** Hear It 🎧
- Play 'Hear It'.
- Say a word and ask the children to hold up fingers to show the number of syllables.
- Try using:
  one syllable – *pin, top, dare, trim, bird*;
  two syllables – *button, stupid, downtown, daughter, salmon*;
  three syllables – *photograph, disaster, remember, agreeing.*

| **NLS objectives for Unit 13** | | | |
|---|---|---|---|
| 3.3.W1 | 3.3.W2 | 3.3.W6 | 3.3.W8 (See Spelling Bank page 16) |

## Part 2 | You need

Big Book page 27; coloured pens; dry-wipe boards or notebooks in pairs

**Whole class**

- Revise what was learnt in the previous session.
- Look at the BBk page and look at the pictures. Decide what they show (*dog*, *cat*, *boat*, *snake*, *snail*, *clock*, *candle*, *slipper*, *football*, *trousers*, *skirt*).
- Ask the children to list, on dry-wipe boards, the words that contain three, four, five or six phonemes. This requires silent segmentation!
- Remind them: Say the word slowly, listen to each sound and say it in your head like a robot, separating each sound (e.g. **st-a-mp**).
- You may wish to do the first one together.
- Once boards have been checked, go through each word together, segmenting and blending the sounds.
- Compose some short sentences using the illustrated words – e.g.
  *The clown lost his slipper and he blamed the dog.*

**Review**

- Segmenting can help us spell. Breaking words into syllables can make longer words more manageable.
- Homework review.
- How many words did the children find in *underwater*? (*under*, *water*, etc.)

**Follow-up homework**

- Children write as many words with the **ai** and **oy** sounds as they can remember.

**Test dictation**

OB Recently I started to help more at home.

A The thieves didn't make any noise.
You have the choice of ice-cream or pancakes.

B To do well in sport you must train a lot.
I always annoy my big brother.

C How much does an elephant weigh?

---

**Snip-snap**    See It 👁✍💬

- In pairs, use dry-wipe boards to try to catch each other out – using 'Look, Say, Cover, Write, Check'.
- Partner A writes down a 'hard' word, checking in a dictionary to make sure it is spelt correctly.
- Partner B looks at the word, says the letters quietly, and tries to visualise it.
- Partner A covers the word whilst B tries to write it down correctly. Both check the result. Then A and B swap roles.

**Snip-snap**    Say It 👄🎵

- Focus on words containing the 'long' vowel phoneme **ai** (e.g. *jay*, *weigh*, *grey*, *snake*, *train*, *steak*, *gauge*).
- You say a word and the children chant like robots, segmenting the sounds.
- Then they sound it out to themselves, and write the word on dry-wipe boards.

# More spelling strategies

---

**Objective for Unit 14**

To use a range of strategies for spelling

---

**Part 1** | **You need**    Big Book page 28; coloured pens; dry-wipe boards or notebooks in pairs; Pupil's Book pages 28–29; PCM 14

**Whole class**

■ Introduce the objective: using different spelling strategies.

■ Make a quick checklist of strategies for spelling a word, e.g. breaking the word into bits, checking by looking/remembering by visualising, using a word that rhymes, using a word that is related in meaning or pattern, using a mnemonic or other memory aid, using exaggerated pronunciation, using common prefixes and suffixes, using dictionaries or a spell-check, asking a friend!

■ Look at the BBk page and say to the children: 'Look at the rhyming spider that is completed. You start from the word in the middle and then think of eight rhyming words. You score one point for a word that rhymes and is spelt the same – two points for a word that rhymes and is spelt differently. Can you fill in all eight legs?'

■ Complete the other rhyming spiders on the page, with the children writing possibilities on dry-wipe boards. They could work in pairs or small teams.

■ As you go along, discuss spelling strategies for words. Encourage children to explain the strategy they use for remembering or finding a spelling.

■ Compose sentences together, discussing spelling strategies if necessary, e.g.
    *The chemist is in the cupboard because the donkey was unwell.*
    *The white computer is careful not to make mistakes.*
    *In the autumn we sail on a cruise.*

■ Introduce the oddbod: *water* – see below.

**Pupil activities**

A:    Match rhyming words and make own rhyming pairs.
B:    Continue a poem with rhyming words with different spellings.
C:    Make rhyming word steps.

Extra challenge: Find rhyming words.

**Review**

■ Good spellers use more than one strategy to help them spell and to help them remember a spelling. Run through the class checklist.

**Homework**

Using words that often go together as a strategy for remembering a spelling.

---

**Oddbod**    water 😑 👁 💭

■ Remember by altering pronunciation to fit the spelling – 'water', saying **wat** to rhyme with **cat**.

■ It sounds as if it should be 'warter' or 'worter' or 'wotter' – these look wrong and have too many letters.

■ Try using the phrase, *To make water, take an* i *from the waiter* as a memory aid.

**Snip-snap**    Does It Look Right? 👁

■ Play 'Right or Wrong' – emphasis on 'does it look right'?

■ You write up a word, spelt in several different ways.

■ Children put thumbs up or down or write on dry-wipe boards the version they think is correct.

■ E.g. you write up *gurl, gril, girl*. Ask the children: 'Which one is it? How do you know?' Discuss ways to remember (see oddbod, Unit 7).

**NLS objective for Unit 14**

3.3.W6

**Part 2** | **You need**     Big Book page 29; coloured pens; dry-wipe boards or notebooks in pairs

**Whole class**
- Revise what was learnt in the previous session.
- Look at the BBk page and together, read the word squares and work out how they are constructed (words read horizontally and vertically).
- Create other word squares in the spaces provided – start with three or four letters and build up.
- Ask the children to contribute ideas for the next word by writing on their dry-wipe boards. (You could invite some children to fill in spaces in the book.)
- Discuss spelling strategies – ways to find a spelling and strategies for remembering. Encourage children to explain their tactics.
- Compose some short couplets using the rhyming words children have generated.

**Review**
- Good spellers use lots of ways to ensure that a spelling is correct – and they double-check.
- Homework review.
- Children swap PCMs with a partner and read the sentences they have written.

**Follow-up homework**
- Children write in their spelling logs the words they had most difficulty spelling, and what strategies they use to help them remember each spelling.

**Test dictation**
- OB  The water in the pool was deep and grey.
- A    Roy felt unwell last night.
  My trousers have a blue belt.
- B    Can anybody shout louder than Chris?
  I like my steak without potatoes.
- C    Mum saw through my story and she knew it wasn't true.

**Snip-snap**   Taking a Picture
- You write a key word in the top left-hand corner of the board. Try: *would, once, went*.
- Ask the children to 'take a picture' of the word, close their eyes and see it.
- Show Me: say, 'Hold it there … Now jot it down and show me.'
- Check the spellings and repeat with other words.

**Snip-snap**   Hear It
- Emphasis on 'hear it' – use of phonics.
- Children sound out words together like robots, e.g. *chick, back, struck, buzz, mess, tax, sun, omit, head, match, coach, clay, indeed, speech, sham, mop, strain, flew, throat, goat, supply, bright.*

# Words in words and homonyms

---

**Objective for Unit 15**

To identify words within words and homonyms

---

**Part 1** | **You need**    Big Book page 30; coloured pens; dry-wipe boards or notebooks in pairs; Pupil's Book pages 30–31; PCM 15

**Whole class**
- Introduce the first objective: words within words.
- Look at the BBk page and, together, look at the first web and underline or circle the different words within *father*.
- Work on each word in turn. Give children time to look and note down words within words on their dry-wipe boards – who can spot the most?
- Discuss with the children how this might help them know how to spell the words.
- Together, compose sentences on the board using some of these words and noticing others, e.g.

  *Father and Mother were pretending that whatever happened, they would behave.*

  *The young police constable thought that he had seen something disgusting.*
- Introduce the oddbod: *wood* – see below.

**Pupil activities**
- A:    Look for words within words.
- B:    Look for words within words.
- C:    Look for words within words and write memory aids.

Extra challenge: Make up long nonsense words.

**Review**
- When spelling, listen for words within words. When trying to remember a spelling it may help to find hidden words, e.g. *There is a **hen** in **when***.

**Homework**    Looking for words within words.

---

**Oddbod**    wood
- Remember the rhyme 'good in the wood'.
- Remember that you have to *look* in a *wood*.
- Draw eyes in the **oo** in *wood* and *look*.

**Snip-snap**    Quickfire Spelling
- Quickfire spelling game. One child starts by saying and spelling a word, e.g. *cart* – c-a-r-t.
- Next child has to say and spell a word that starts with the last letter of *cart*, e.g. *train*.
- This gets passed on, working from the final letter in the previous word, until one child spells a word wrong or can't think of one.
- This could be played as a class, in teams or in pairs.

> **NLS objectives for Unit 15**
> 3.3.W8        3.3.W14 (See Spelling Bank pages 16, 20)

## Part 2 | You need        Big Book page 31; coloured pens; dry-wipe boards or notebooks in pairs

**Whole class**
- Revise what was learnt in the previous session.
- Introduce the second objective: looking at words which have the same spelling but different meanings (homonyms).
- Look at the BBk page and, together, read the sentences and tease out their meanings. Ask children to tell you which words are homonyms, and circle them.
- At the bottom of the page, write more silly sentences together, using the list of homonyms given.
- Children could invent sentences on their dry-wipe boards – read some aloud if enough children manage this.
- Discuss different meanings of the words in context and how they may be a different word class, e.g. *leaves* (noun) – things on trees; *leaves* (verb) – doesn't take away.
- Compose some sentences (or use children's examples) using homonyms – e.g. *The wind blows but he* leaves *the* leaves *on the trees*.

**Review**
- Some words have one spelling and several meanings.
- Homework review.
- Start with a small word like *in* and add letters gradually to make larger and larger words.

**Follow-up homework**
- Children make a note of one of the silly sentences they made with homonyms. They then look for words within each word.

**Test dictation**
- OB  The foxes ran through the scary wood.
- A    The boys had a terrible fight.
       The moon was very bright last night.
- B    Bill felt lonely without his dog.
       What has happened to your new shoes?
- C    Dad has to catch the train to go to work.

---

**Snip-snap**    What's the Meaning?
- You say a word, e.g. *book*.
- Children write a sentence using the word twice, with different meanings, e.g.
  *Can I book a time to read this book?*
- Try: *age, fit, form, ring, sound, pop, stand, letter, spot, flat, table, safe, foot, dear, last, yard.*

**Snip-snap**    Spot the Hidden Word
- Write up a key word (e.g. *then, more, been, help, good*).
- Show Me: children quickly look for a word within the word and write it on dry-wipe boards (e.g. *then* – he).

# 16 Prefixes

## Objective for Unit 16

To use prefixes mis, non, ex, co, anti

**Part 1** | **You need**    Big Book page 32; coloured pens; dry-wipe boards or notebooks in pairs; Pupil's Book pages 32–33; PCM 16

**Whole class**
- Introduce the objectives: using prefixes – ask who can remember what these do.
- Look at the BBk page.
- Ask the children to match each prefix to its definition, and explain their reasoning.
- Draw lines from the definitions to the balloons. Write up other words with these prefixes that the children can think of.
- Together, compose sentences on a board, using words with these prefixes, e.g.
  *It was my* mis*fortune to* mis*behave and* re*quire* anti*biotics.*
  *I have* co*-written some* non*-fiction but it is an* anti*climax.*
- Children should spell by letter patterns, but if any do ask why the ex words do not leave a free-standing English word, explain that these words come from a different language (Latin). Note also that some ex words leave what appears to be an English word that in fact means something quite different (e.g. *claim* in ex*claim* is from Latin *clamare*, 'to shout').
- Introduce the oddbods: *your, you're* – see below.

**Pupil activities**
A:    Identify real words with prefixes and write sentences.
B:    Supply the correct prefix.
C:    Supply the correct prefix.

Think about …: Discovering prefixes' meanings by studying words they are used in.

**Review**
- Recap what has been learnt – prefixes alter the meaning of the root word, but do not change its spelling.

**Homework**    Sorting words with prefixes from those without.

---

**Oddbods**   your, you're
- *you're = you are*. The apostrophe takes the place of the missing a from *are*.
- *Your* is used in a similar way to *our* – *your* book belongs to *you*, *our* books belong to *us*.
- To know which spelling is needed, think about the meaning. Could the word be replaced by *you are*?

**Snip-snap**   Creating New Words
- You write up the prefixes mis, non, ex, co and anti, then write up a base word, e.g. *judge*.
- Children write on dry-wipe boards the root plus prefix, e.g. *misjudge*.
- Try other words, e.g. *behave, place, deed, lead, use, count, hear, read, take, stop, stick, sense, change, claim, star*, etc.

---

**NLS objectives for Unit 16**

3.3.W9          3.3.W10

---

## Part 2 | You need   Big Book page 33; coloured pens; dry-wipe boards or notebooks in pairs

**Whole class**
- Revise what was learnt in the previous session.
- Look at the BBk page and read through the adverts. Look at how word roots have had their meaning altered by adding a prefix.
- List some more dislikes and problems, e.g. *fear of spiders, homework, rain*.
- Invent some slogans together, e.g. *'Scared of spiders? Try anti-spider spray ...'*
- Ask the children to invent new words for the slogans, writing on dry-wipe boards, e.g. *non-homework*.

**Review**
- When we add on these prefixes, the spelling of the word root does not change. Prefixes alter the meaning of the word root.

- Homework review.
- Use a dictionary to discover the meanings of the prefixes you found in the Homework exercise.

**Follow-up homework**
- Children make a note of what mis, non, ex, co, and anti mean.
  mis means 'wrong'; non means 'not' or 'opposite of'; ex means 'out (of)'; co means 'together (with)' or 'joint'; anti means 'against'.

**Test dictation**
OB Your boat leaves in one hour from now.
A   Viv was trying to mislead me.
    Mrs Ball misread the answer.
B   The girls disappeared through the exit.
    "That's not true!" exclaimed Ben.
C   At school we are taught to co-operate.

---

**Snip-snap**   Prefix Charades
- Children work in pairs, one acting out one of the words that has a prefix while the other tries to guess it.
- For instance, for the word *antifreeze*, one child could mime being extremely cold, and then draw a cross in the air. (Try: *non-stick, misread, anti-clockwise, co-pilot*.)

**Snip-snap**   Quickfire Writing
- Quickfire writing, joining up the letters of mis, non, ex, co, anti.
- Try it with eyes closed.
- Who can write a prefix ten times in 30 seconds?

# More prefixes

---

**Objective for Unit 17**

To use knowledge of prefixes in spelling

---

**Part 1** | **You need**    Big Book page 34; coloured pens; dry-wipe boards or notebooks in pairs; Pupil's Book pages 34–35; PCM 17

**Whole class**
- Introduce the objective: using prefixes to help spelling.
- Give a quickfire reminder of the work on prefixes from the previous unit.
- Look at the BBk page – the house of prefixes and the house full of base words.
- Take a prefix at a time and ask the children to make a 'real' word or create new ('nonsense') words.
- Look at the meanings. List other words that share the same prefix.
- Write invented or real words into sentences on the board, e.g.
  *Hippos are* anti-*clean.*
  *The summer is* in*cool.*
  *Man is a* bi*legged animal.*
- Introduce the oddbod: *school* – see below.

**Pupil activities**
A:    Combine prefixes and root words.
B:    Combine prefixes and root words, and use them in sentences.
C:    Create opposites by using prefixes.

Extra challenge: Find the meanings of other prefixes.

**Review**
- Recap the meanings of the prefixes covered.

**Homework**    Match the prefixes to their meanings and find words.

---

**Oddbod**    school 🤔💬
- Easy enough – rhymes with *fool*! *Go to school, and you won't be a fool.*
- Whales and dolphins come in '*schools*' too!
- Links to *scholar, scholastic, scholarly, scholarship*.

**Snip-snap**    Quickfire Questions 💬✏️
- Choose a letter, e.g. i.
- You ask a question – children write down answer – immediately!
- Lose a point if you use the letter!
- Try to gear the answers to the questions to words with prefixes, e.g.: What do you use to speak to someone in another country? (*Telephone/ e-mail/video link*, etc. – only *telephone* doesn't lose a point.)

> **NLS objective for Unit 17**
>
> 3.3.W10 (See Spelling Bank page 18)

## Part 2 | You need

Big Book page 35; coloured pens; dry-wipe boards or notebooks in pairs

**Whole class**
- Revise what was learnt in the previous session.
- Look at the BBk page and read the advert through, explaining the meanings of any difficult words.
- Cross out the prefixes, then re-read it.
- How does this alter the meaning? (creates opposites)
- Extract the prefixes that create opposites – un, il, im, in, ir.
- Together, compose sentences on a board, using prefixes to create opposites, e.g.:

  *The unheated rooms are unfit for patients and impossible to use. Your writing is illegible, the spellings are incorrect, and I'm unable to give you any marks.*

**Review**
- A prefix is a small group of letters that goes on the beginning of a word and changes its meaning, e.g. *kind/unkind*. This can help with spelling. Generally, neither the prefix nor the root word changes in spelling.

- Homework review.
- For each of the prefixes on the PCM, think of a word that uses it and make a note of it.

**Follow-up homework**
- Children make a note of the prefixes from the PCM and their meanings – they should use this when spelling.

**Test dictation**
- OB My bigger brother leaves school in July.
- A Tom had outgrown his grey jumper.
  You go through the exit to get outside.
- B I doubt that Mum will overlook my mistake.
  I can understand why Bev is successful.
- C I feel disloyal but that girl is always up to mischief.

---

**Snip-snap** Change the Meaning
- You write up prefixes that make opposites: un, il, im, in, ir.
- Then you say a base word, e.g. *perfect*.
- Children select one prefix to create a word, e.g. imperfect, and say the new word.
- Try using *pleasant, legal, perfect, visible, regular, kind, logical, possible, correct, replaceable.*

**Snip-snap** How Much?
- You write up some words with number prefixes.
- Ask the children to guess at their meanings.
- Try: bi ('two'), tri ('three'), centi ('hundredth'), micro ('millionth', or just 'small'), milli ('thousandth')

# More apostrophes

---

**Objective for Unit 18**

To investigate more words with contraction apostrophes

---

**Part 1** | **You need**    Big Book page 36; coloured pens; dry-wipe boards or notebooks in pairs; Pupil's Book pages 36–37; PCM 18

**Whole class**

- Introduce the objective: using apostrophes in contractions. Ask the children whether they can remember what these are and what they do.
- Ask for a few suggestions of contracted forms from previous units (10 and 11), e.g. *can't*.
- Mention particularly the cases of *won't* (introduces letters that weren't in the full form) and *shan't* (letters omitted at places other than where the apostrophe falls).
- Look at the BBk page and read the newspaper headlines together.
- Circle the contracted words with apostrophes.
- Write the full forms in the boxes provided, e.g. *he's = he has*. Alternatively, children can write on their dry-wipe boards.
- Together, compose sentences or more newspaper headlines, using contracted forms, e.g.

  > *Goldilocks **won't** pay up!*
  > *Wolfie – **he's** at it again.*
  > ***I'm** going out and **I'd** like you to come.*

- In preparation for the Extra challenge, remind children that an apostrophe takes the place of a missing letter or letters and is not the joining of two words, e.g. in *salt n' vinegar* the apostrophes replace a and d in *and*.
- Introduce the oddbods: *push, pull* – see below.

**Pupil activities**

A:    Rewrite contracted forms in full.
B:    Rewrite contracted forms in full.
C:    Rewrite sentences to make them more formal by using the extended form.

Extra challenge: Supply the missing letters in contracted forms.

---

**Oddbod**    push, pull 👁 👂 ✍ 💭

- Both start in the same way, pu – remember them as a pair.
- Emphasise the end sounds **sh** and **l**.
- Children speed-write both words, getting used to the feel of the spelling.
- In Dr Dolittle there is an animal that has a head at either end – it is called a 'Pushmi-Pullyu'. This may help to make the spelling memorable.

**Snip-snap**    Write in Full ✍

- You call out a contracted word, e.g. *can't*.
- Children speed-write the full form and hold up their dry-wipe boards, e.g. *cannot*.
- Try using: *you're, we'll, she'll, you've, we've, she'd, I'd, I'm, shan't, wouldn't*.

---

**NLS objective for Unit 18**

3.3.W11 (See Spelling Bank page 19)

---

**Part 2** | **You need**     Big Book page 37; coloured pens; dry-wipe boards or notebooks in pairs;

**Whole class**
- Revise what was learnt in the previous session.
- Look at the BBk page and read out the passage, circling the apostrophes.
- Write up the full forms of the first two contractions on the board. Children contribute by writing on dry-wipe boards what the rest of the full forms should be.
- Point out the case near the end (*Haven't you* becomes *Have you not*) where the words in the full form have to be re-ordered so that they sound natural.
- Read the original passage again, then read the version substituting the full forms for the contractions. Ask children which sounds more formal and what is the effect of using a contracted form. (It makes language sound less formal – more like speech than writing.)

**Review**
- Apostrophes are used to show that letters are missed out. Contracted forms make language sound chatty.

- Homework review.
- What do you notice about words like *he's*, *she's* and *they'd*, *we'd*? (Can mean *is* or *has*; and *had* or *would*.)

**Follow-up homework**
- Children make a list of words with contracted forms that might be difficult to spell, e.g. *o'clock*, *would've*.

**Test dictation**
OB  "Don't push me!" exclaimed Dan crossly.
A   I've been in trouble before.
    I'll return to school in September.
B   He's the funniest boy I know.
    You've been very unkind and disloyal.
C   They're always giggling and smiling but we aren't.

---

**Snip-snap**   Quick Contractions
- You call out a full form, e.g. *have not*.
- Ask the children to speed-write the contracted form on dry-wipe boards – with the apostrophe in the correct place, e.g. *haven't*.
- Try using: *does not, do not, will not, should not, they had, we had, she has, I have, they are, he is*.

**Snip-snap**   Finding Oddbod Rhymes
- Write up a key word (try: *back, just, so, now*).
- Children call out a rhyme.
- Score extra points for rhymes with a different letter pattern (e.g. *so, know*).

# Counting syllables and spot the error

**Objectives for Additional Unit 1**

To identify syllables and incorrect spellings in own writing

**Part 1** | **You need**   Big Book page 38; different-coloured pens; dry-wipe boards or notebooks in pairs; Pupil's Book pages 38–39; PCM A1

**Whole class**
- Introduce the objectives: breaking words into syllables to make spelling easier and spotting incorrect spellings in own writing.
- Begin the session with a quick reminder about syllables – clap out names as a class.
- You clap a person's name – the children put thumbs up if it has the same number of syllables as their name.
- Look at the BBk page. Ask the children how many syllables each word has. Sort the words into three groups, and use a coloured pen to underline the syllables – use different colours for two-, three- or four-syllable words.
- Discuss how breaking words into syllables can help spelling. It makes a longer word more manageable to break it into bits, and in lots of words the syllables are spelt the same.
- To show this last point, go back to each word and notice how other words may share their first, last or middle syllables.
- Write a few nonsense sentences and use syllabification to aid spelling, focusing children's attention onto different parts of the words, e.g.
  *On Monday a peanut went to play football at the seaside.*
  *On Sunday an elephant went for a ride in a helicopter.*
- Introduce the oddbod: *even* – see below.

**Pupil activities**
- A:   Join up parts of words to create words and sort by number of syllables.
- B:   Work out the number of syllables in dinosaur names.
- C:   Describe months with an adjective with the same number of syllables.

Extra challenge: The longest English word.

**Review**
- During and after writing, check for words that are incorrectly spelt.
- Break words into syllables – slow the word down – tap the syllables, to help with spelling.

**Homework**   Generate words containing ant and sort them by the number of syllables.

---

**Oddbod**   even
- **ven** rhymes with **men**.
- Use a mnemonic: *even Steven*.
- List other words that rhyme, e.g. *men, pen, hen, ben, ten*.
- Just remember that it starts with a simple e.

**Snip-snap**   Isolating Syllables
- Dictate two-syllable words.
- Children isolate and write down the final syllable only, e.g. *hum-**bug**, slow-**ly**, birth-**day**, al-**ways**, bed-**room**, snow-**man**, blis-**ter**, writ-**er**, win-**dow**, sun-**set**, play-**ing***.

**NLS objectives for Additional Unit 1**

3.1.W4        3.1.W5

### Part 2

| **You need** | Big Book page 39; different-coloured pens; dry-wipe boards or notebooks in pairs |

**Whole class**
- Revise what was learnt in the previous session.
- Look at the BBk page.
- Read through the text, circling any words that the children suggest do not 'look right'. Point out any they have missed.
- Use a range of strategies, double-checking with other strategies, to correct the spelling errors.
- Include tapping words out into their syllables as a handy method.
- Encourage children to try out spellings in pairs on their dry-wipe boards – then check to see if they 'look right'.

**Review**
- During and after writing, check for words that are incorrectly spelt.
- Break words into syllables – slow the word down – tap the syllables, to help with spelling.

- Homework review.
- Ask the children if they can think of any more *ant* words to add to their columns.

**Follow-up homework**
- From their own writing, children add spellings of words that they often get wrong to their spelling log. They should make notes about how they will remember them.

**Test dictation**
OB   August is even hotter than July.
A     Mum would like a bigger handbag.
        Their news was not that important.
B     Pip went up the stairs to her bedroom.
        Not much happened on that grey afternoon.
C     The thieves were reluctant to co-operate.

---

**Snip-snap**   Sort Out the Letters 👁
- Play the game, 'Muddled Letters'.
- Break a word down into its letters then mix the letters up.
- Ask: Who can guess the word and write its correct spelling the fastest? The only clue is the number of syllables, e.g.
  *iglr* – one syllable (*girl*).
  *eoplpe* – two syllables (*people*).
  *alrte* – two syllables (*alter* or *later* or *alert*).
  *hfiins* – two syllables (*finish*).

**Snip-snap**   Spot the Error(s) 👁 ✒
- You write up words with mistakes in them.
- Tell the children how many mistakes there are in each.
- On dry-wipe boards, the children write each word correctly; e.g. the following all have one error to put right: *jokeing, runing, slowley, undoo, crys, shurt, groe*.

# Even more spelling strategies

**Objective for Additional Unit 2**

To use a range of strategies for spelling

**Part 1** | **You need**    Big Book page 40; coloured pens; dry-wipe boards or notebooks in pairs; Pupil's Book pages 40–41; PCM A2

**Whole class**
- Introduce the objective: using different spelling strategies.
- Look at the BBk page and remind children of the game 'Prefix Fans'.
- For each prefix, ask children to supply base words to make new words.
- Time Out/Show Me: Children make other combinations on dry-wipe boards.
- Remind children that they need the whole of the prefix and the whole of the base word.
- Draw attention to any words which need a hyphen.
- Tease out spelling points and strategies that arise. Refer to the objective to help identify different strategies.
- Compose sentences together, testing different strategies. This might relate to other parts of the curriculum being studied.
- Introduce the oddbod: *next* – see below.

**Pupil activities**
A:    Create word fans for prefixes.
B:    Create word fans for suffixes.
C:    Create words that use both a prefix and a suffix.

Extra challenge: Find and write homonyms.

**Review**
- Reminder of different strategies for spelling words, e.g. identifying common prefixes and suffixes.

**Homework**    Spelling by analogy with common words with like spellings and writing a rhyme.

---

**Oddbod**    next ⊚ ✍ ⊚
- Take a mental 'photo' of this one.
- Children practise writing it in turns, chanting the letters. When one child has finished writing, call out 'Next!' to the following one.

**Snip-snap**    Change the Word 🔊 ✍
- Play a word-changing game. Relate the chosen words to the term's objectives, or to words the children often spell incorrectly.
- You write or say a word. Children write as many words as they can think of, changing one letter at a time, e.g. you say 'light'; children write *light, might, night, tight, sight, fight, fright.*

---

**NLS objective for Additional Unit 2**

3.2.W6

---

**Part 2** | **You need**     Big Book page 41; coloured pens; dry-wipe boards or notebooks in pairs

**Whole class**
- Revise what was learnt in the previous session.
- Look at the BBk page and play the 'Balloon Game'. Tell children: 'In the balloon there are a number of precious things. Each time you make a mistake another thing drops out!'
- You read the sentences. Children write on dry-wipe boards what they think is the correct spelling, choosing from the underlined words. These are all spellings that often get muddled.
- Discuss what strategies they have used, e.g. it looks right, *hear* includes the word ear, etc.
- If most children have given the wrong answer, an item is lost from the balloon.
- Discuss strategies for remembering these spellings. Ask those children who got it right to explain to the others how to remember them.
- The 'Balloon Game' can be used again for other words that you provide.

**Review**
- Create a class reminder list of different ways to remember a correct spelling.
- Homework review.
- Make a note of any words that you were unsure of in the 'Spelling sets'.

**Follow-up homework**
- Starting with the following words, children see how many related words they can build. They can use dictionaries to help if they get stuck: *light* (e.g. *lighter, lightning, lighting, lighten,* etc.), *hand, sea, way, air.*

**Test dictation**
OB  Let's sit next to the exit.
A   I'm always prepared to help my brother.
    We saw a preview of the big match.
B   Sal opened her bag and started to unpack.
    He's playing happily outside with Pam.
C   They've predicted bad weather for the weekend.

---

**Snip-snap**   Letter I-Spy
- Play 'Letter I-Spy'.
- This is exactly the same as traditional I-spy, except you say a starting letter and the children have to guess the word one letter at a time.
- To win, children have to guess each letter in turn and then put the segments together to make a word.

**Snip-snap**   Anagram Hangman
- Play 'Anagram Hangman'.
- You write up a word with the letters jumbled.
- Children have to guess letters in order – give them the first letter if they find it difficult to get started.
- Everyone has a go at the same time. Child scores a point for being first to guess the right letter.

# Learning spellings and proofreading

<table>
<tr><td colspan="2">Objectives for Additional Unit 3<br>To identify mis-spelt words; practise new spellings</td></tr>
</table>

**Part 1** | **You need** — Big Book page 42; coloured pens; dry-wipe boards or notebooks in pairs; Pupil's Book pages 42–43; PCM A3

**Whole class**
- Introduce the objectives: identifying mis-spellings, and using 'Look, Say, Cover, Write, Check'.
- Look at the BBk page. Make some words together – starting with one letter and choosing appropriate middles and endings. Write the words on the board and see how many can be made.
- Pose a challenge, e.g. 'How many words can you spell that end in st, using only the letters on the page, in one minute?' 'How many words can you spell that end in es?' etc. Children write on dry-wipe boards.
- Help the children to notice how some letters or letter patterns most often occur in certain places in words, e.g. x is usually not at the beginning, ly is often at the end, etc.
- Together, discuss and list strategies for learning new and hard words. Discuss strategies that different children use. Keep the list handy. Example strategies might be:
  Words that go in pairs – *push* and *pull*.
  Use rhymes and repeating patterns – *mur/mur*.
  Silly sayings – *shoe* – S*am* h*as* o*range* e*ars*.
  Words related by meaning – *hear, ear*.
  Words related by letter pattern – *feat, beat, seat*.
  Remembering words within words – *There's a* hen *in* when.
  Knowing a rule – ing most often comes at the end of words.
  Asking a friend or relative.
- Introduce the oddbod: *when* – see below.

**Pupil activities**
A:  Build words from word roots plus suffixes.
B:  Build words from prefixes plus word roots plus suffixes.
C:  Build words from letter groups.

Extra challenge: Make words from the word *Cambridge*.

**Review**
- Recap the list of different strategies for remembering and working out spellings.

**Homework**
Inventing acrostics as memory aids.

---

**Oddbod**   when
- Relate to asking questions – and other question words – *who, where, when, why* and *what*.
- Write it, joining the letters.
- Take a photo in your mind's eye – write it down.
- Chant '**w-h-e-n**' rhythmically.
- Use a mnemonic, '*There is a* hen *in* when'.

**Snip-snap**   Does It Look Right?
- You write up two or three options for words that are often mis-spelt, e.g. *wur, wer, were*.
- Children jot down on dry-wipe boards the one that 'looks' right.
- How else do they know – rhyme, prefix, suffix, mnemonic, etc.

---

**NLS objectives for Additional Unit 3**

3.3.W5      3.3.W7

---

## Part 2 | You need      Big Book page 43; coloured pens; dry-wipe boards or notebooks in pairs

**Whole class**
- Revise what was learnt in the previous session.
- Focus on the BBk page and tell the children that the writer of this letter has made some mistakes – their job is to spot the errors and correct them.
- Read through the letter. Take it slowly, line by line.
- Children point out the word(s) that they think are wrong – circle these. They then try to spell them correctly on dry-wipe boards.
- Discuss strategies for getting the correct spelling. Get successful children to explain how they knew a correct spelling.
- Play at being the 'spelling agony aunt'. List the spelling errors and give a way of remembering/knowing the spelling. Remember to include the 'Look, Say, Cover, Write, Check' routine, plus other strategies for different words.

**Review**
- Think about the main strategies for how to spot spelling mistakes, and about how to achieve correct spelling.

- Homework review.
- Swap acrostics with your friends and make your collection bigger.

**Follow-up homework**
- Children should decide always to proof-read at least the first ten lines of their writing. If they are good spellers, they should make it more!
- Children find their last long piece of writing and check the first ten lines. Can they see any mistakes? If so, they should correct them.

**Test dictation**
OB  When was your youngest sister born?
A    I taught my little brother to hop.
      Joe was hopping in the playground.
B    Unfortunately I answered incorrectly.
      Who is the best football player?
C    "You're going to be late!" shouted Dad impatiently.

---

**Snip-snap**   Word Squares
- Show the children how to invent a word square, using three-letter words.
- Show them how to write the first word, e.g. dot:
  D O T
  O
  T
- Now they have to think of a three-letter word starting with t, e.g. ten:
  D O T
  O E
  T E N
- Show Me: ask the children to write their own three-letter word squares on their dry-wipe boards.

**Snip-snap**   Anagrams
- Play 'Anagrams'. You write jumbled-up words and give clues to what they are.
- Children use dry-wipe boards to sort out correct spellings.
- Children, in pairs, give each other an anagram to solve. To make it easy, underline the first letter each time.
- Try: in a slam (animals; clue: 'things with four legs and often a tail'); ideals (ladies; clue: 'people who are female adults'); hugs lint (sunlight; clue: 'brightness from the sky').

# Facsimile Big Book pages

This section contains facsimiles of the Big Book pages for ease of planning.

## 1 'Long' vowel phonemes and sounding out

Part 1

Read these words and listen to the vowel phonemes.
What is the difference?

cat   care   got   goat

Say the underlined words slowly.
What is the vowel phoneme in each word?

Imagine a ...

Imagine a soap.
Slip on a slope.

Imagine a crow.
Lost in the snow.

Imagine a snake.
Eating some cake.

Imagine a snail.
Wagging a tail.

Imagine a tray.
Covered in hay.

put

Part 2

Match the pictures to the words.
List the most common ways to spell the **ie**, **ee** and **oo** phonemes.

seat   fly   sweet   stew   moon
tie   tune   feet   fight   light   blue
spoon   pie   stream   cry   light

Listing **ie**, **ee** and **oo** sounds

| ie | ee | oo |
|----|----|----|
|    |    |    |

## 2 adding

Part 1

All these verbs have had **ing** added to them.
What has happened to their spellings?
Sort them into two groups.

jump — jumping
dive — diving
leap — leaping

smile — smiling
catch — catching
shake — shaking

Adding ing

| just add ing | drop e and add ing |
|----|----|
|    |    |

was

Part 2

Which words belong in which postbox?

slip   joke   clap   shout   give   try   move   come
bet   enjoy   rain   call   stop   shut   arrive

just add ing

double the consonant and add ing

drop e and add ing

## 3 endings

Part 1

Find the rhyming pairs.
What do the words have in common?

double   pickle
prickle   fable   goggle
toggle   rubble
table   paddle   cuddle
saddle   muddle
bubble   trouble

they

Part 2

What happens to the spelling of these words if you add on another ending?

tickle   double
giggle   cuddle

| adding ly | adding ed | adding ing |
|----|----|----|
|    |    |    |

## 4 Common prefixes

Part 1

Change the underlined words by adding un or re.
How do the meanings change?

### The kind king

Once a friendly king wanted to visit the seaside. When he arrived, he decided to build a palace on the clean beach. He had to call all the trained builders.

They were able to write to their families about what a lucky time they were having.

To pay for the bricks the king king had to sell some popular camels. He wanted to turn the seaside into a paradise for his happy family.

The king decided to pay the lucky builders by giving them and their families a comfortable holiday

are   our

Part 2

Change the underlined words by removing, or changing, the prefix. How does this alter the meaning?

### The disloyal servant

There was once a king who loved to bounce. He had an unhappy servant who did not like to bounce at all. The servant disliked his job and was very displeased with the king

He decided to let the air out of the King's bouncy castle and then disappear. It was dishonest and he knew that he should not disobey orders, but he was discontent

However, the king had suspected this servant for some time. So the king had taken the unusual step of filling the castle with jam! The servant disconnected the air supply and pricked holes all over the castle. When the jam started to spray everywhere, the servant felt very uncomfortable, most unhappy and looked rather unwell! He looked a bit like a jam doughnut!

# Facsimile Big Book pages cont.

Find the matching pairs.

How has the prefix changed the meaning?

d sobey          far          untidy

well          happy          pleasant
              unhappy

un fair          obey

do disappear          tidy          dislike

like          appear          connect

dis connect          unwell          undo

          unpleasant

moment

---

Change or get rid of the prefixes and put the crooks on the wrong track

### Secret Message

Follow these instructions carefully. To find the gold you must go to Danger Hall. Disobey the sign that says "Beware". Begin by walking anti-clockwise round the building, until you reach a statue. At this point discontinue walking down the path. Follow the small track through the trees, till you reach the shed. It is impossible to enter the shed. First you must disconnect the alarm.

Make sure that you stay invisible at this point. Disconnect the red and blue wires. Push the button. Decrease the pressure as you push or the box might explode.

Now you can unfasten the shed door. Outside the shed, you will find the key in a flower pot. Unlock the door.

Good luck.

A friend

---

### Shannon's game

i  j  k  l  m  n  o  P  q  r

h          s

g          t

f          u

e          v

d          w

c          x

b          y

a          z

out

---

### Scorpions

Most p____ fear scorpions, but they are actually only l____ creatures. However, not m____ of us k____ much about them. T____ are related to spiders. Both have e____ legs and t____ bodies are divided into m____ parts. Also, both of them hunt their prey, which they p____ with a sting.

Scorpions have a large pair of pincers that act like c____ for g____ their prey. They can g____ up to 15 cm long. They live in warm, d____ countries a____ the world.

---

Circle the **or** and **er** phonemes.

### Mrs McGinty

Mrs McGinty kept a pet stork.
She trained the big bird
To whistle and talk

Mrs McGinty spoke not a word.
She sat in a tree
To hoot like a bird

Mrs McGinty started to purr.
She kept herself clean
By licking her fur.

Mrs McGinty held out a paw.
She patted me gently
And dug in a claw.

Mrs McGinty sat on the floor.
She chewed on a bone
And let out a roar.

girl

---

Circle the **air** phonemes.

### Scary stairs

In the air          On the stairs
I had a scare,          I sold my wares,
I saw a pair          Got some stares
Of floating pears.          From hairy hares.

At the fair          On the stairs
I made a dare          I saw the bear
I saw a bare bear          Eat the pears
Standing there.          But they were square!

---

What do you notice about these words?
They are called calligrams.

tall taller tallest

silly sillier silliest

fat fatter fattest

hot hotter hottest

long longer longest

thin thinner thinnest

crazy crazier craziest

hairy hairier hairiest

first

---

Sort these words into groups.

| just add y | drop e and add y | double the consonant and add y |
|------------|------------------|-------------------------------|
|            |                  |                               |

bone          smell          fuss

cheek          sun          stone          mess

fun          full          nut          crisp

water          fat          grease          laze

          smoke

**46**

# Facsimile Big Book pages cont.

9

Underline all the plurals. Sort them into two types, depending on whether s or es has been added.

Through the bushes, the foxes ran, while crashes of thunder broke around them. The owls sat in bunches in the tree branches, sheltering. The hiss of the rain hitting the pond water startled the frogs. The policeman wished that he was at home with his kids, playing with their games and comics, cars and bikes, rails circling the room for the toy trains to run on. Instead, he was out looking for robbers in the cold dark night.

Sort these plurals into four types.

| Spelling plurals | | | |
|---|---|---|---|
| es | ies | ves | s |

watches    boxes    dishes    hooves    cakes

cities    parties    calves    knives    trees

scarves    parrots    passes    toys

babies    halves    moons

armies    wishes    horses

last

10

Read these examples.

| foot | + | ball | = | football |
| light | + | house | = | lighthouse |
| earth | + | quake | = | earthquake |
| shoe | + | lace | = | shoelace |
| bed | + | room | = | bedroom |
| goal | + | keeper | = | goalkeeper |

Build compound words around these words:

| time | fish | eye |
|---|---|---|

clue

Join the monster to its correct hat!

11

Underline the words with silent letters. Sort them into two types.

## The gnome and the knight

The gnome gnawed his knuckle and gnashed his gnarled teeth. A gnat sat on his knee. He tried to undo the knot that tied his feet but in the end used a knife.

Just then a knight appeared. The gnome had to kneel. His knees were knocking. He did not know what to do. "Oh knickers!" he muttered.

| Silent letters | |
|---|---|
| gn | kn |

answer

Look for words with apostrophes. Can you make them disappear? What happens to the words?

## Ennio and the gnome

"Don't make a sound," muttered the gnome, ducking down.

"I can't see and I wouldn't miss this for anything," hissed Ennio. The gnome frowned at his friend. "We shouldn't attack them. We haven't waited long enough. It won't be easy."

The gnome shook his head. "They've got swords! We're unarmed. It won't be funny if we're captured."

"But the crown's mine," whispered Ennio. "They'd never dare harm me. It'll be easy."

"You've got us into enough trouble!" the gnome snapped back.

12

Make as many combinations of a base word and a suffix as you can.

friend + ly = friendly
friend + less = friendless

**Base words**

| hope | home | care | time | sick |
| rich | cold | cheer | lone | read |

**Suffixes**

y    ful    et    ly    less    able

HAVE A GO

Add the suffixes to the words.

careful    mad    kind    ly    funny    slow    quick    friend

forget    ful    wish    hope    pity    hate    pain    sorrow

thank    end    care    less    speech    job    fear    thought

lovely

# Facsimile Big Book pages cont.

## 13 | More 'long' vowel phonemes and sounding out

**Part 2**

Sort the **ai** (ai, ay, a-e) and **oy** (oi and oy) words by their spellings.

### The chimpanzee

One day a young boy found a chimpanzee in his garden. He thought it was a toy at first, but the chimp was not a toy. It had run away from the zoo and it didn't want to be played with like a toy. It was looking for happiness. It climbed a tree and lay down for a snooze. It soon forgot all about the boy.

"I may never get another chance to play with a chimp, I'm going to enjoy myself," thought the boy. He was soon beginning to make stupid noises. Of course, it was silly to annoy a chimp, but I'm afraid that he was a boy of very little brain.

The chimp woke up feeling annoyed. The noise made him feel angry. It had 'to avoid or destroy the noise. The chimp had no choice so it jumped from the branch and chased the boy back into the house. The boy's mum had to call the zoo keepers to catch the chimp.

help

---

**Part 2**

Sound out these words in 'robot-speak'. How many sounds in each word?

**96**

water

---

## 14 | More spelling strategies

**Part 1**

rough
enough    stuff
gruff   fluff   bluff
tough   cuff
buff

Find rhymes for some more rhyming spiders.

said        buy

feet        ring

**98**

---

**Part 2**

Look for words in the word squares.

```
D O G   C A T S   S L I C E
I   O   O   O     E     A
G E T   S U N S   N   A L
                  S A N D Y
```

Make some more word squares.

**99**

---

## 15 | Words in words and homonyms

**Part 1**

Look for smaller words for each web.

fat    the
at     he
a      her         father

brother        otherwise

whatever

something

wood

---

**Part 2**

Circle the homonyms.

My mum waves at the waves and leaves the leaves on the land where they land.

I left my left arm in the left luggage.

Stick this stick in the ground, and then stick on this notice so that people will notice it.

Train the bride how to get her train on the train.

Now write your own sentences using these words:

sink    trip    arms    match    fan    rock
back    light    club    bank    snap    rose

HAVE A GO

**31**

---

## 16 | Prefixes

**Part 1**

Match each prefix to its meaning.

anti
anti-freeze
anti-clockwise
anti-aircraft

mis
misbehave
misprint
mistake

non
non-stop
non-stick
non-fiction

ex
exit
extract
explode

co
co-star
co-operate
co-written

'against'        'wrong'

'out (of)'

'not' or 'opposite of'    'joint' or 'together with'

your    you're

**30**

---

**Part 2**

Use the prefixes mis, non, ex, co and anti to create some new adverts.

| Dislikes and problems | Possible slogan |
|---|---|
| Sneezing | **Anti-Sneeze** keeps you free |
| Burnt food | **Overcooked?** Turn to Non-burn Sauce. |

**33**

# Facsimile Big Book pages cont.

## 17 More prefixes

Part 1

Join the prefixes and the base words.
Which words can you make?

**Prefixes**

re – again
anti – against
in – not or within
pre – before
non – not
inter – between
ex – out (of)
un – not
mis – wrong, or wrongly
dis – not, or out of
over – too much
up – up
under – below, or less than
out – beyond or not in
multi – many

**Base words**

| | |
|---|---|
| lock | write |
| take | dead |
| turn | grow |
| smoking | place |
| side | clean |
| sleep | kind |
| act | view |
| play | press |
| live | sided |

school

## For sale

Part 2

The builders have been irresponsible. The plumbing is irregular and unfit for humans. The wiring is illegal. The flat is insecure. The doors will unlock easily and the windows unfasten with no problems.

Do not be put off by the stairs. They are impossible to climb!

The neighbours are most unhelpful and impolite. They will make you feel completely unsettled.

There is an unpleasant view from this untidy flat. The mountain roads nearby are indescribable.

We are flexible over the price of £30,000.

## 18 More apostrophes

Part 1

Circle the apostrophes.
Write the words in full, without an apostrophe.

They've crashed again!

We're ready for winter.

He's the winner!

stick 'em up!

push    pull

Part 2

Circle the apostrophes. Write the words out in full, without an apostrophe.

"I'd been shopping. I hadn't got much and wasn't goin' to wait for a bus. So, I'd just started to walk. I can't remember too much. They'd come running round the corner and grabbed a handbag from a young woman. As it happened I thought, 'She's screaming, he's rushing after them and they've cleared off.' I've never been so scared in my life. Haven't you tracked the robbers down yet? I'll be amazed if they've got away with it."

HAVE A GO

---

How many syllables do these words have? Sort them into three groups. Use different colours to highlight words with two, three or four syllables.

behind tomorrow Friday loudly amazing birthday giant yesterday sandy distant always elephant September computer today because begin moving tonight Saturday bewildered sand inside sandwich also already merrily helicopter

even

## ZOO SPIDER SCARE

Circle the mistakes.

Large mice experts from the Brompton Zoo were watching for one of their prize exhibits. A large South American tarintula has escaped from its cage. The cage was made of reinforced glass.

The spider's bite is poisonous and police are afraid that a mite could...

with the long hands. The spider is about the size of a tennis ball, is black and hairy.

"If anyone sees a spider of this description they should report it to the police at wance.

"Do not approach it as it is armed and dangerous," said Inspector Crumble of Brompton Police.

---

Max Prefix Fun

lock    inter

miss    go    under    store

next

nunt    sense

## The balloon game

Choose the right spelling. If you make a mistake, you'll lose something from the balloon!

We out/are happy flying so high.

We brought/bought a cat for catching mice.

The captain does not out/know the way.

I think I can here/hear air escaping!

We told the birds to clear off/off.

I asked Mrs Fright if she would like to/to come two/too/to.

There/their is only one map and we do not want to lose it.

---

How many words can you spell that start with:
wh-, f-, sh-, pl-, sp-, gl-...continue with...

when

---

Circle the mistakes

Dear Agony Aunt,

I am having trouble becos my spelling is not very good.

I am writing to ask you for sum advice. Wen I right I have lots of good ideas but the spelling is not always correct. I was hopeing that you wood be able to give me some good weighs to remember hard spellings. I no that my teacher would be grateful.

Best wishes,

Charlie

How can Charlie learn and remember the spellings?